"A lively and persuasive case for genuine shareholder democracy to make businesses properly accountable."

"A lively, lucid, bracing and brilliantly forthright love letter to everyone who believes in the principles of democratic capitalism. It should be essential material for anyone who has a pension or investment account, or is a student of economics – and is a must-read challenge for the City of London and corporate leaders today."

"How should we 'reform' capitalism? Merryn Somerset Webb, one of our best financial journalists, is a powerful and persuasive advocate of 'shareholder democracy'. With 11 million people owning shares, directly or indirectly, she argues it is time for the individual owners of Corporate UK to assert their rights and empower themselves. Her manifesto explains how this can be done and capitalism transformed."

"Merryn is one of the clearest thinkers and communicators in finance. In this brilliant and concise book she explains why many people are disillusioned with capitalism; why they're wrong to be; and how we can make it even better and fairer than it already is. A must read."

"A breezy, accessible and admirably brief summary of what the stock market is, how it works, and where it isn't working well enough."

Merryn
Somerset
Webb

SHARE
POWER

This paperback edition published in 2023

First published in the UK in 2022 by Short Books
an imprint of Octopus Publishing Group Ltd
Carmelite House, 50 Victoria Embankment
London, EC4Y 0DZ

www.octopusbooks.co.uk

An Hachette UK Company
www.hachette.co.uk

10 9 8 7 6 5 4 3 2 1

A CIP catalogue record for this book is available
from the British Library.

ISBN: 9781780725628

Cover design by Richard Green
Author photograph by Phoebe Grigor

Printed and bound in Great Britain by Clays Ltd, Elcograf S.p.A.

This FSC® label means that materials used for the
product have been responsibly sourced

For Dot and Art — who I hope will use
their share power well

Contents

Introduction 9

1. What is a company? 17

2. Making everyone an owner 30

3. If you are the owner, why don't you feel
   like it? 44

4. Where have all the companies gone? 58

5. Who's asking and who's telling? 73

6. What would be different if we could
   use our votes? 95

7. Some progress 115

8. The way forward 133

   Glossary 144

   Acknowledgements 150

   References 152

INTRODUCTION

There have been many experiments with socialism over the last 100 years. To date, every one of them has ended in poverty and pain. Yet if you ask a person under 40 in the US if they would call themselves a capitalist, the odds are they will say no. Ask in the UK and you might get a similar response: in 2019 some 30% of voters in the general election opted for a self-confessed (if remarkably ineffectual) socialist, Jeremy Corbyn. So what's going on? It's partly about the passing of time: the horrors of Mao's China and the Soviet Union have lost their resonance – for the under-40s at least. But it's also about a disconnect in modern capitalism: too many people feel out of touch with the workings of the economy and have lost any sense of control over how it works. The big companies that were once respected as the drivers of our growth and hence our wealth are now regarded with suspicion.

That makes the socialist idea of common ownership sound better than it should. It also makes now – post-pandemic – a good time to argue for change, for governments to tax and spend their way to wealth equality and for the giant corporates that dominate economic activity to be better and do better.

Everyone wants the global economy of the future to be somehow superior to that of the past – and in particular to the pre-pandemic economy. There's much talk of demanding more from our big companies – insisting that they focus less on making profits for shareholders and more on the good of the communities with which they interact. Companies, we are told, should act on climate change and diversity; they should care more about their suppliers and their customers; they should watch over employee mental health; and attempt to vanquish the gender pay gap. And if they won't do these things themselves, the state and "communities" should somehow force them into it. More sanctions, more regulations and more nationalisation.

But here's the thing. It isn't governments or fund managers that own the world's big companies – and therefore they shouldn't really be the ones to dictate how those companies interpret "good" and "bad". The truth is that we own the companies and we should be the ones telling them how we want them to behave; essentially how we want capitalism to be reset (assuming we do – it isn't a given).

What do I mean when I say we own them? In the UK,

pretty much everyone (in work at least) now owns shares in our listed companies. Two and a half million people have their own stocks and shares Individual Savings Accounts (ISAs). Two million people have opened self-invested personal pensions (SIPPs) inside which they tend to hold shares in one form or another. Anyone over 22 years old who is employed and earning over £10,000 will have been auto-enrolled into a pension scheme by their employer (you can opt out but very few people do). And all these pension schemes hold shares. Most developed countries will have a similar system, although the UK's is particularly good. So one way or another, we are all effectively part owners of the corporate world. That common ownership people say they crave? We already have it. Every share we own comes with a vote over company decisions; everything from executive pay to who gets to be on the board of directors and any major shifts in corporate goals or strategies. What if we were to use those votes? Fed up with companies letting themselves be sold abroad? We can vote against it. Not convinced that an oil company should spend billions becoming a renewable energy company instead of just winding down and paying out the cash? We can vote against it. Angry with a mining company that has caused pollution in the rivers around its sites? We can vote against its directors keeping their jobs. The transformation of capitalism is – technically at least – in our gift.

I say "technically" because, as ever, the devil is in the

detail. When the limited company was first invented, you knew where you were at with your shares. You had a certificate noting your ownership and rights and you exercised them as you liked (or sold the certificate on as you liked). As recently as 1963, more than half of the shares in the UK stock market were held like this – by individuals. Those individuals had paper share certificates for each holding and were regularly contacted directly by the company's executives (with annual reports on performance and the like). These were the days of individual shareholder activists such as the Gilbert brothers, who, at their peak, owned stakes in 1,500 companies and spent their lives going around the annual general meetings (AGMs) of those companies, haranguing management about things they didn't like. One of them kept a clown's horn with him so he could blow it every time a CEO said something he considered silly (happy days – more on the brothers in Chapter 7).

Now only 13.5% of UK shares are individually owned and, for the few who have them, there is no bit of paper, and mostly no annual report. We hold our shares digitally on investment platforms (such as Hargreaves Lansdown and Interactive Investor in the UK) and need to be very proactive if we want to use our votes at the AGMs of the companies we invest in. The rest of the UK's shares are owned either by international investors or (and this is the crucial bit) by pension and fund managers. Instead of taking on the responsibility of choosing, buying and managing shares, we have increasingly given our money to fund managers and asked them to do it for us. We don't hold the shares ourselves. We hold units in the funds that hold the shares. There is some good news among all this, of course. Back in 1963 only 3% of the population were shareholders (about two million people). Now at least 75% of employees are. Nonetheless, the result is that we have effectively delegated our voting rights to the nation's fund managers – and in particular to pension fund managers.

This isn't unique to the UK – it has happened in the US and in Japan too. But everywhere it creates the same problem. We remain the ultimate owners, but we have no power – so instead of making us part of the show, our shares are effectively nothing but a ticket allowing us to watch it (if we can be bothered). Fund managers (a smallish group of very well-paid, mostly group-thinking men – female fund managers remain in the minority) speak for us to the managers of the companies we own and vote for us. And those fund managers very rarely ask us what we want them to say or how we want them to vote. That needs to change – and can change. The stock market is in one sense now hugely democratic – we all own it – and hugely undemocratic – only very few of us get a say on how it is run. The technology exists to allow fund managers to hand the votes our shares come with back to us – all we need to do is persuade them to use it. It's simple: we all tell the fund managers how we want to vote, they aggregate and vote accordingly. Only that way can we use our voices to make sure that we get the capitalism and the (buzzword alert) "stewardship" we want (whatever that turns out to be).

There is a view that capitalism has failed – and that it needs somehow to be totally transformed. My desk is littered with books explaining the miseries caused by capitalism; some offering radical solutions for saving it or reimagining it. It's mostly nonsense. First, capitalism has demonstrably not failed. It is instead a stunning success – as you would expect given that it works naturally with the human instinct for improvement and accumulation. The facts speak for themselves: in the early 1990s some 35% of the world's population lived in extreme poverty. It's now under 10% – and, although the pandemic has stalled things a little, the number continues to fall.

If you find yourself questioning the brilliance of the free markets, think of how Western economies reacted to the pandemic. Aside from the few days when supermarkets ran out of loo paper and pasta, there were no shortages of anything. You might have felt the world had shut down as you were furloughed or settled in to work from home for a year, but it did not. The wheels kept turning – and companies adapted to keep their shows on the road. Logistics firms expanded, restaurants switched to home delivery and physical retailers moved online. Across the world, the rate at which new businesses started up soared. Companies came through. There's a message in there about the power of technology and innovation in free markets – and however you cut it, there is no doubt that capitalism passed the test of 2020 with flying colours (unlike governments by the way – but that's another book).

Corporate capitalism is far from perfect. Big (and small) companies often behave badly. But as a system it works brilliantly. What we need to do is re-engage with it, not reimagine it. That means taking up our responsibilities as owners, criticising the companies we have stakes in if necessary but also supporting them as they produce the products and services that help us. We also need to remind ourselves that there isn't really a "them" and an "us". We are all customers, employees or suppliers in one way or another – and we are also mostly owners. The great reformers of capitalism like to make a clear distinction between stakeholder and shareholder, but in the main, the two are one and the same. If we can remind people that they are all owners and convince them that they have the power to act as such (by using their votes as shareholders), we can reconnect big business and ordinary people while also forcing better behaviour on the corporate world.

The good news is that since I first started thinking about all this – and even since the first edition of *Share Power* was published, much progress has been made. There is increasing recognition among ordinary investors and fund managers that power must be shared. The small groups trying to facilitate that are gaining significant traction. And most interestingly of all, Larry Fink, head of the world's largest asset manager, BlackRock, has come round to my way of thinking. In November last year he announced a pilot scheme to allow ordinary individual investors with money in funds run by BlackRock to vote on contested proposals at AGMs. Technology, he said, was allowing him to help enable "a revolution in shareholder democracy" that would "transform the relationship between asset owners and companies." Exciting times!

There is however a long way to go from one company kicking off a well-meaning pilot scheme to full shareholder democracy for all. We need to keep the momentum going. In the next eight chapters I will explain how we can all work to do just that.

1

WHAT IS A COMPANY?

It seems like an absurd question, doesn't it? Everyone knows what a company is. There are two million in the UK alone,[1] for heaven's sake – and ten million plus in the US.[2] It seems simple enough – a company is an organisation that sells stuff to make money. Everyone either works for one, owns some of one or uses things made or provided by one. But there is more to it than that. These companies are the building blocks of our economies – without the structure they give all of us and the legal and financial protection they give their founders, the global economy would be an entirely different animal. A much less efficient and probably very much poorer one. Think of them as the superpower of capitalism – a kind of killer app for economic progress (and most other progress along the way).

Where did companies come from, and how have they

changed our world? For a good 300,000 years – most of human history – we had no use for them. Until very recently, most wealth was tied up in land, which was owned by the monarch, the Church or the aristocracy. Most commercial arrangements were short term, fairly individual and, beyond some land tenancy arrangements, certainly not designed to last beyond the lifetimes of those involved. The very rich had estates and occasionally operated in family partnerships. There's some evidence of people clubbing together in the ancient world (think 2000 BC)[3] to finance the odd shipping cargo, but most in the commercial sector operated as sole traders. This only began to change as the world opened up – and ambitious individuals wanted to get involved in projects that had obvious potential, but that weren't either one-off (in the way that banding together to finance a commercial cargo was) or just too expensive (or risky) for one family to finance alone. But doing anything money-related in groups without set parameters to work within is not easy – as anyone who has ever tried to divvy up a restaurant bill between 10 people will know. For everyone to feel confident in group financial activity, a resilient legal structure was needed. And this had to achieve two things. First, it needed to allow lots of different investors to share the risks and rewards of a project over a reasonably long time (without endlessly falling out over how to manage it and how to share out the cash). And second, it needed to provide a way for the

ownership of the business to change as the original investors aged and died or just wanted to hand their interest on
– without the business itself being affected by the change.

The innovation that accomplished all these things was
the company, and in particular the "joint stock" company –
so called because its assets (the stock)[4] are jointly owned by a
group of investors. The first of these companies were established in Europe – mostly in prosperous northern Italy. But
the earliest well-documented one seems to be the Société
des Moulins du Bazacle, formed by a group of 14th-century
flour mill owners near Toulouse in southern France. Their
aim was to harness the power of their local river to drive
their flour mill.[5, 6] Building the dam they needed to get the
project going was far too expensive for any one of them,
so rather than setting the whole thing up with a series of
individual deals and contracts, they created a novel profit-
sharing agreement. Everyone put money in. In exchange
they each got back a piece of paper noting the percentage
of the costs paid and entitling each of them to a similar
percentage of the mill's profits, paid annually (we now
call these annual payments "dividends"). That might not
sound madly exciting. But the next bit was. Investors were
able to sell these bits of paper to whomever they wanted,
whenever they wanted. Their price – just as with contem-
porary shares – varied in line with each year's profits, as
did the dividend which was originally paid "in kind" – i.e.
in flour. This meant that the ownership and the operation

of the mill were separated – it was possible for someone with no social or geographical connection to the original constructors of the project to be an owner. That led to the thing that really set the Société des Moulins du Bazacle apart from all previous trading and banking groups. It had a board of directors. These men could make decisions on behalf of their shareholders but without consulting them.[7] The company used this power when it decided to switch to paying dividends in cash in 1840, for example, something for which those without much capacity to trade flour must have been heartily grateful. This was a big step. One of the problems of jointly owned assets is too many opinions. What if all the owners want different things? The board is the solution to this. The board represents the investors and has a duty to maximise their overall returns – and to take the best collective decisions to do so (whatever individual investors might want). This all worked brilliantly: the Société des Moulins du Bazacle turned out to be nearly immortal. It ground wheat from 1372 to 1886 and even now the hydroelectric plant that is its legacy is part of one of France's big energy companies.[8]

From the longevity of the Bazacle mill alone you can see just how well this kind of risk pooling can work. But there was a way to make it even better. The early companies, such as the mill, had one whopping – and vital – difference from the many millions of companies on the go around the world today. They were "unlimited" companies. That meant that the owners' liabilities were uncapped. They were entitled to their share of the company's profits, which was good. However, if things went wrong (and the fact that the Bazacle is such a rarity offers a few hints as to how often they did – and how brave the world's first shareholders were), as "unlimited" shareholders they were also responsible for all the liabilities of the company, including the payment of all its debts. So if you had put, say, £100 into a company, and then found it went bust with debts worth £500 per share, you'd not only lose your £100 but be on the hook for the £500 too. Not so nice. That meant that even as it became possible for people to invest in projects they weren't connected to or weren't able to have proper physical oversight of, it still wasn't a madly good idea. The solution? One of the greatest conceptual innovations of all time: the limited liability company. With these, your losses as a shareholder became limited to the amount you originally invested – in the example above just the £100. You would of course not want the company to fail – and would be keeping a close eye on those hired to run it (the directors). But if it were to fail, as a shareholder your only problem would be the loss of your stake. That its debts might not be paid back in full would be a problem for those who had lent to it (and a risk they understood when they made the loan). This might sound like a small change. But it wasn't. With losses capped, investors could take on more overall risk – investing in more companies and creating economic growth along the way. This changed everything. Without the structure, and the organisational capacities of the limited company, says *Financial Times* columnist Martin Wolf, "the unprecedented economic development seen since the middle of the 19th century would have been impossible". Who would have put up the money for, say, the crazy-sounding ideas of the original railway entrepreneurs, the internet start-ups and the likes of Tesla if they had thought they would lose their house in the process? No one. But knowing they could lose only their original stake made it much more attractive. If you are looking for the key invention that created the modern world, the limited liability company might be the one to go for.

Not everyone was mad for the limited liability idea. Early observers thought it scandalous that investors might ever be able to walk away from losses and be protected from any negative consequences of an activity they facilitated. They also worried that the structure would cause conflict between shareholders and company managers: if they were to want different things, who would prevail? Adam Smith in his wonderful book *The Wealth of Nations*, published in 1776 (and a bestseller at the time), did not seem completely convinced.

"The directors of such [joint-stock] companies, however, being the managers rather of other people's money than of their own, it cannot well be expected, that they should watch over it with the same anxious vigilance with which the partners in a private copartnery frequently watch over their own... Negligence and profusion, therefore, must always prevail, more or less, in the management of the affairs of such a company."[9]

Luckily, while Smith has turned out to be right in many of his criticisms (as we'll see in later chapters), his disapproval came too late. By then the rise of the company and the introduction of limited liability (which gradually became their structure of choice) had met with another innovation – the stock exchange, a place where investors could gather to trade the bits of paper (now known as shares) that represented their fractional ownership of companies. This development was obvious in hindsight; if a company didn't have a limited life, how could investors cash out if they could not pass their shares, and the rights to collect dividends from those shares, to someone else? You could have bought and sold shares before this but there was no set system for doing so. From 1602, when the Dutch East India Company listed on the new Amsterdam Stock Exchange, there was.

This combination of innovations kicked off a few hundred years of experimentation, excitement and, of course, the odd bubble/bust cycle. The most well known was the South Sea Bubble,[10] in which overexcited investors bid up the shares of the company from £100 to £1,000, only to see it collapse, ruining most of them along the way.

But my favourite (in that it comes with the best stories) was the Diving Bell Bubble of the late 1600s. This started with the stunning treasure recovery efforts of one William Phipps. Phipps knew where a "richly laden Spanish plate ship" had been wrecked and, after one failed attempt to find it, persuaded the Duke of Albemarle to put up the majority of the cash for another go in 1687. They formed a small joint stock company and Phipps headed for Hispaniola. There, just as he was giving up and calling in the last boat ("provisions were running low"), a diver popped down to grab a piece of seaweed one of the men was interested in (or so the story goes). The diver saw the shape of a gun on the seabed, "operations were then pursued vigorously" and Phipps's ship sailed home with 32 tons of silver and jewels worth roughly £250,000 (well over £50m in today's money). His original investors made a return of around 10,000% on their shares, something that triggered the birth of scores of companies named specifically after their intentions – two classic examples being The Company for Recovering Treasure from Wrecks off Bermuda and The Company Created for Recovering Treasure from Wrecks in Other Places Granted to Thomas Neale.

Things got a bit more sensible in the 19th century with the advent of the railways. The vast cost of building them meant that they really did need the limited liability format to get going. Rail companies used it well: shares were sold on the stock markets, money was raised and thousands of miles of track laid. By 1871, there were 45,000 miles of rail routes in the US.

These railway companies became the first ever major employers (national armies aside), requiring management – often retired military men – to ensure trains could move around the country without crashing into one another and to oversee large numbers of employees: in 1891 the US army, navy and marines employed nearly 40,000 people; the Pennsylvania Railroad alone employed over 110,000.[11] Modern accounting and information systems developed with the railways, but crucially, the railway companies were also the first modern publicly quoted companies – of the type we recognise today. Until the 1890s, Wall Street almost exclusively financed US railroads, which caused trading on the nascent New York Stock Exchange to take off – the first **million-share volume day** was in 1886. The stock market limited liability listed company had come of age.

Next came the big manufacturing companies. In 1901, Andrew Carnegie sold his steel business to J.P. Morgan and Elbert Gary for $480m.[12] They rolled up another 200 smaller firms and sold the resulting giant, U.S. Steel, with 67% of US steel production,[13] to the public at a valuation of $1.4bn – equivalent to $44.5bn today. The public company really had arrived both in the US and in the UK. By 1956, when *Fortune* produced its first ever list of the world's large corporations, they were mostly in the US and mostly manufacturing companies – three in steel and three in cars (General Motors was the largest).[14] Today the companies on that list (as in those that list their shares for sale on the stock market) are more facilitators or platforms than manufacturers. Amazon is, to a large degree, a market place. Facebook is a content conduit and Apple a technology design company. But the names you know are just the tip of a very deep iceberg. In the US there are 4,400 listed companies. In the UK there are around 2,000. Worldwide there are well over 40,000.[15] Not all companies are listed on stock markets. We refer to those that are as "public companies" (in that anyone can turn up at any time and buy a share). Those that are not listed are known as "private companies". They have the same sort of structure (they can be owned by lots of different people at once and they are limited liability) but their shares aren't available to buy and sell on public stock markets.

So here we are, 800 years on from the formation of the first company-type organisation and what we have ended up with is very different from what we started with. The first companies had obvious owners, set purposes and limited lives. A big listed company today will have many thousands of owners (over 50% of the shares in UK companies are owned by foreign entities, for example). It will have no fixed purpose (what it does can chop and change) and it can technically be immortal. It's also an entity in its own right. When you deal with a company you effectively deal with a "nexus of contracts" that make up a corporate personality.[16] It is not a person or even a group of people but an entity that we treat as a person, in that it can own assets, enter contracts and be sued. Think of it perhaps in terms of the old philosophical question of the axe. If you change its head is it still the same axe? That's the easy bit. If you now change the handle is it still the same axe? Hard to say, isn't it?[17] Not so with a company. It could change its location, change its business (Toyota started as a textile machinery manufacturer), change every employee. But it would still, legally at least, be the same company. The same perpetual entity.

The modern company is also often enormous. A wave of mega mergers from the 1980s onwards, combined with the stunning technological innovations of newer companies such as Apple and Amazon, has given us economies dominated by giants. Two firms control 90% of America's massive beer market. Four operators run most of America's airline industry.[18] By 2021, the total market value of Apple (the sum of the value of all its shares in issue) came to more than the value of most countries' GDP.[19] Our world is dominated by these huge listed companies, companies that have fingers in every pie of all our lives. They have significant power to do good – and to do bad. Here's Edward, First Baron Thurlow, picking up the nub of the potential problems back in the late 1700s: "Corporations have neither bodies to be punished nor souls to be condemned, they therefore do as they like."

So here is the real question, the one that really matters and will make the difference to all of us over the next few decades: who owns these companies? And who has the rights that go with owning them? The public sector aside, these companies effectively *are* the economy, so ownership of them gives you both access to the wealth created by that economy and, to some degree, control over how that economy works – this could be in the sense of how much people are paid and where goods are sourced from, or in the sense of how much renewable energy is used in the creation of goods and services. Tesco and Compass Group are the largest non-public sector employers in the UK: more people work at Tesco than in the army, HM Revenue and Customs, the Department for Work and Pensions and the Royal Air Force combined. While there are many millions more small companies than big, globally many more of us work for big companies than small (47% vs 34% in the US in 2017).[20] In the US, the total profits made by companies as a percentage of GDP are higher than they were in 1929 – a point at which the political world was extremely worried about the dominance of corporate giants. At the same time, the McKinsey Global Institute calculates that 80% of global economic profits are generated by only 10% of companies.[21]

There is a real concentration of power here. So who owns them and who controls them? The first part of the answer to this is that it might be you; in fact, it probably is you. That's a good thing – more in Chapter 2. The second part is that it isn't you – it's company management and big institutions. That's probably a bad thing. More on this in Chapter 3.

2

MAKING EVERYONE AN OWNER

In the 1980s, Margaret Thatcher had an idea. She believed in free markets – and in the ability of companies to be a global force for good. She wanted everyone to feel the same. And the best way to do that? She reckoned it was to make them shareholders – to sell them shares in the UK's nationalised companies and so give them a tangible stake in corporate Britain as part owners of it. That would make them engage with capitalism (the good and the bad) and ensure they reaped some of the most obvious rewards of its success – dividends paid out by money-making companies to their owners. She did a pretty good job.

A huge number of companies were state owned in 1970s Britain – think Thomas Cook, Cable & Wireless, Rolls-Royce, Jaguar and British Steel. They all moved to the private sector – some £60bn worth of them.[22] Every possible incentive was used to encourage people to apply for shares – including high dividend yields and egalitarian limits to how many shares anyone could apply for (usually 100–200).[23] Older readers will remember the "Tell Sid" campaign, in which TV ads and billboards all over the country showed people telling other people to apply for shares in British Gas. It went about as viral as anything could go pre-internet: by the end of Thatcher's 1980s privatisation programme, the number of individual share-holders in the UK had risen from three million to around nine million people (15% of the population), many of them with nice little portfolios of newly privatised companies. Given that only around 3% of the population held shares at all in the 1960s, that's quite something.[24] As an aside, it is worth noting that the privatisation of all these companies – BT, British Airways, BAA, the National Grid etc – didn't just raise a one-off lump of cash for the Treasury; it also provided long-term tax revenue. In 1979, the aggregate deficits of the nationalised industries cost us the equiva-lent of 3p in income tax. By the 1990s, not only were all the services they provided much better and cheaper (in the 1970s you often had to join a waiting list to get a phone line installed) but they were "producing handsome tax revenues for the Government".[25]

The result? More successful companies owned by more people. Win-win! Well, sort of. The problem was that while it was undeniably a good thing that smaller inves-tors were able to hold little portfolios of shares, in the main they didn't do much more than that. There was, says stock market historian John Littlewood, "no evidence that privatisation created a new culture of individuals owning shares in companies across the stock market".[26] It was hard – and expensive – to get financial advice and holding any investments was an admin-heavy business. Lots of small investors turned out to be shorter-term thinkers than was hoped: most of the newly floated companies saw their share prices rise on the first day, making "stagging" (applying for the shares and selling them at the end of the first day) a popular activity. People who did this ended up with a nice new car or holiday abroad – but not with a share portfolio. Mrs T had made a start – but one that didn't make quite the impact she had envisaged.

If only Mrs Thatcher – and Ronald Reagan, who firmly agreed with her on the benefits of widespread participation in stock markets – could see us now. Share ownership has been on the up in much of the West: in 1989, 31% of US families held shares; now, thanks to the 401(k) pension savings schemes that kicked off in the 1980s and 1990s, more like 55% do – with an average holding of around $40,000.[27] But it has been in the UK where the numbers have shown the most stunning of transformations.

When Mrs Thatcher left office, most pensions were in what are called defined benefit schemes. These guaranteed you an annual pay-out of a percentage of your final salary linked to inflation every year until your death.

They were brilliant (and, should you be a public sector worker still getting one, they very much still are – lucky you). They were also very expensive for employers – we live an awful lot longer now than when these pensions were first created. So they have mostly been phased out. As they went, they left a lot of people high and dry – no one wants to have no pension provision if they think they might live to 95. The solution was the defined contribution pension, which relies on the individual building up money inside a pension wrapper (see glossary) and hoping to live off the proceeds in retirement. It's not as good as a defined benefit pension, but as long as you actually do the required saving, it works pretty well. You can, I think, guess the problem. Most people never did the saving part, and certainly never enough of it.

Enter pension auto-enrolment. In 2012, the government introduced a system under which every single person in work in the UK earning more than £10,000 and over 22 years old is automatically placed in a pension savings scheme to which they contribute 5% of their income and their employer chucks in at least another 3%. If you don't want to save in this way, you have to say so – and opt out. Like all successful policies, this relied on apathy and admin aversion. I am a classic example here: I will do anything, literally anything, not to have to fill in a form. The result? Since 2012, the number of workers who hold shares via their company-sponsored pension plan has risen from

10.7 million to nearly 20 million people. In 2012, 46% of workers had workplace pensions – now nearly 80% do (in 2020, 88% of those eligible remained opted in).[28] If you are 25 today and on the average income of around £30,000, you should have some £250,000 saved by the time you hit retirement (as long as nothing goes horribly wrong in the economy or the stock market – not a given, by the way). Suddenly, the health of individual companies to whom you might think you have no connection matters to you. And so do markets as a whole. This is a trend that is unstoppable: as the years go past the value and volume of the assets held in this way are going to build and build. And this comes with a fantastic consequence: whether they know it or not, almost everyone with a job in the UK has a stake in corporate UK – just as Mrs Thatcher hoped they would.

But the world of pensions is just the beginning of today's shareholder story. A pension or 401(k) plan is only one way to hold shares. In the UK, you can hold them in an ordinary trading account or in a variety of other tax-efficient wrappers such as an Individual Savings Account (ISA) – around 20 million people in the UK save into an ISA (although a large number of these are held in cash, not shares).[29] The real news, however, is not about these wrappers or tax efficiency. It is about the sudden rush of enthusiasm for investing in shares during the Covid pandemic. In 2020 and 2021, something remarkable began to happen.

Ordinary people (many of whom probably don't know they already have equity-based pensions) began to engage with stock markets. Investment platforms and stockbrokers everywhere started to report sharp rises in the number of new accounts and the volume of trade. In the US, the fund manager Fidelity added 3.7 million accounts in 2020. In the UK, a run-through of the established brokers suggests that some 400,000–500,000 new trading accounts were opened in early 2020. That doesn't sound huge relative to Mrs Thatcher's privatisation programme. But it represents a huge uptick in business for them and doesn't include the numbers from newer players. Share trading site eToro, which was only founded in 2007, saw a 30% increase in the number of traders on its site in 2020, from 13 million to 17 million.[30] By mid 2021, that was up to 20 million. At the end of 2019, instant trading app Robinhood (which launched in the US in 2014, offering commission-free and almost admin-free trading across the market) had 10 million users. By May 2020 it had 13 million and by mid 2021, 31 million.[31] Another US company, OTC Markets Group, which runs platforms that facilitate trading in smaller companies, reported that its trading volumes were up fourfold in January 2021 relative to January 2020. "We have seen significant increases in participation from retail [private] investors," one of its vice presidents told the *Wall Street Journal*.[32] Interest has been on the up elsewhere around the world too. In Japan, the number of accounts being opened by individual investors soared during 2020.[33] In Korea, private investors are now the dominant force in the market – accounting for around 60% of daily turnover. According to the *Financial Times*,[34] some 52% of South Korea's population at least "dabble" in stocks. They are, says the MD of Petra Capital, a Seoul-based investment firm, "becoming a powerful force".

In general, all these new investors are rather younger than the big investment companies are used to.[35] Hargreaves Lansdown, the UK's biggest retail investment platform, notes (with some incredulity) that the average age of a new client is down from 45 to 37. Interactive Investor, another influential UK investing platform, has observed something similar: in the last three months of 2020, 25% of their new clients were under 35. Overall, the average age of a UK trader fell by 12.5% in 2020, to 36 – 35 for men and 38 for women. There's much of the same from Alliance Trust; 66% of 18–34-year-olds who responded to one of their surveys said they started investing in 2020. No wonder Hargreaves Lansdown started producing social media ads featuring young tattooed women in 2021. How times change.

But their age is not the only thing about new investors that would boggle Mrs T's brain. Lots of them operate far from the established platforms I have my pension on. They have a higher risk appetite than previous investors: surveys show that they are 50% more likely to buy individual stocks than funds and that they have a heavy tech bias. They aren't shy of the old guard either. When investment old-timer Charlie Munger, best known as sidekick to one of the greatest investors of all time, Warren Buffett, told Robinhood traders they had the "mindset of racetrack betters", they told him to "mind your own business grumpy gramps". They are twice as likely to buy cryptocurrencies as equities (this is something Charles Schwab tells us only 8% of the over-50s do – I'd be surprised if it was that high). They buy and sell in a flash. They share screenshots of their portfolios. They trade fractions of shares. They are heavily influenced by their peers and by social media. They get their investing information from TikTok, Twitter, Reddit boards[36] and now even "rooms" on Chatroom. There is a wild west of information (misinformation?) out there. The investing hashtag on TikTok has 1.4 billion views and the personal finance one has nearly 4 billion.

One to watch to see how it works? Try Taylor Price (find her @pricelesstay). She is from New York, she's in her early 20s and she calls herself a "financial activist".[37] I could watch her for hours (nice music, smart production values, good hair). I'm not alone. She has over one million followers and almost 20 million likes (only a few are mine... honest). She is a "finfluencer" – a financial social media influencer or perhaps a "stock jock".

New investors also follow each other's actual trades (very sharing economy). Look up Jeppe Kirk Bonde (@

jeppekirkbonde). You can find him trading on eToro – where 40% of the new customers who have signed up since last March 2021 are under 30. Twenty-three thousand people follow his trades, which he tells them have made him an average annual return of 30% a year since 2013. (If that were sustainable it would be a historical first...).

All this adds up – in 2020, 20% of trades in the US and the UK came from retail (private) investors. Larry Fink, the CEO of BlackRock, the world's biggest fund management business and a firm that saw $129bn worth of new money flow into its coffers in the third quarter of 2020 alone, said there was "a record amount of retail participation in the marketplace".[38] (More on Larry later.) Estimates in 2021 put retail activity at about 20–25% of the market for the year.[39] That's double 2019 and more than all hedge funds combined. The man-on-the-street investor has been on the rampage[40] – and, as it happens, having rather a lot of fun along the way.

Back in early 2021, a group of traders, egged on by their participation in a nine-million-member-strong Reddit chat group (Reddit WallStreetBets forum – r/wallstreetbets), worked together to buy shares in and push up the prices of GameStop, a probably past-its-best, US-listed video game retailer. The shares started the year at $17 and hit $483 (up 2,700%) before crashing again. At one point they went up 1,000% in a matter of days – causing eyewatering levels of financial pain to a few hedge funds who had shorted the shares. On one day in January, GameStop was the most traded stock on the planet. Later they had a go at Nokia, Hertz, AMC and even the global silver market. Not for the faint-hearted – particularly given that most of these shares come down fast once the bandwagon moves on. But pretty amusing – watching the whole thing cheered up my second lockdown no end.

These new investors might not stick, of course. Most of them do not come with a thorough knowledge about markets – the *Financial Times* reported in March 2021 that one of the most common questions from newcomers deciding to use Robinhood is "what is the stock market".[41] A large number of new investors tended to be adding investing to existing hobbies such as video gaming and online sports betting. Anyone unconvinced about this should look up Dave Portnoy on Google immediately. The founder of Barstool Sports is the poster boy for sports fans-turned-day traders in the US. One survey in the UK shows that 14% of those who are trading more than they did before say they are doing so because they actually have the time. They are also bored: 11% of those trading say they are doing so because they can't bet on live sports as they used to. There's a reason half of the investors in the US were new to markets in 2020.[42] Perhaps now lockdowns have ended, they will find their old hobbies are more engaging than their new. Without furlough – or the US equivalent of super-generous unemployment and stimulus payments[43] – how many investors will really have time to keep thinking about stock markets? They may also just run out of money.

Think of the pandemic savings so many people made. With money still coming in but expenses newly low, most countries saw sharp rises in their savings rates. Pre-pandemic consumers in the US were able to save 7% of their incomes. By the end of 2020, they had saved 26%. In the UK, that number was 28% and in the EU, 26%. That's a lot of money burning a lot of holes in a lot of pockets. But it's over now: even by the third quarter of 2020 savings rates were back into the teens.[44] The final factor that might turn out to have called time on the fashion for trading is losing money. In the end, investing isn't really supposed to be about memes and trends and pissing off hedge funds. Nor about just buying shares representing the brands you like best, or even cryptocurrencies. Instead, it should be about the long haul of steady growth and dividend collection.

Investing also involves being able to take the rough with the smooth. Note that the market was abnormally profitable during the pandemic years – everything with a compelling story attached to it went up and up again. But stories aren't the same as profits, and one day as much money as has been made – maybe more – will be lost. We need only look at the day traders who took the pain of the 2000 dotcom crash: not many of them stuck around for more. The UK's regulatory body, the Financial Conduct Authority, worries about this. Their surveys show that around 40% of "self-directed investors" with less than three years' trading experience do not consider "losing some money" as one of the risks of investing, while 80% of them also agree with the statement that "There are certain investment types, sectors or companies I consider a safe bet". Yikes. I've got 25 years' experience and there are no types, sectors or companies I consider a safe bet.

All that said, there is more good news than bad here. Much, much more. I suspect those new to the market have rather more stamina than the FCA thinks they do. In April 2021, the much-hyped initial public offering (whereby an unlisted company offers shares to the public for the first time) of food delivery company Deliveroo was a bit of a flop in the UK. The shares (overpriced by overconfident investment bankers – an old story) fell 28% on the first day. The next day, the private investors were back in. UK investment platform Hargreaves Lansdown saw a "surge" in buying from retail investors. It's also worth checking out trader slang for a bit of reassurance: lots of Reddit traders take pride in their "diamond hands" – their ability to hold their positions when they get painful. After all – unlike the losers in 2000 – this lot are of an age where, should they wish, they can afford to be in it for the long term. The Robinhood crew may find that shifts in interest rates and markets make things less fun over the next few years than they have been over the last few. But a good number of them may also hang around. I hope they do.[45]

But go back and look at the numbers at the beginning of this chapter: even if some recent investors drop off, it is worth remembering just how much new money has gone into markets via more conventional routes. Take the US fund management giant Vanguard. It only offers long-term investing vehicles: but in the same week of January that GameStop hysteria was reaching its peak, it saw a threefold jump in new customers compared with the same week the year before. Analysis from Freetrade in the UK also showed that in April 2021 (a busy month for individual trading) seven out of 10 of the top holdings of younger investors were exchange-traded funds or passive funds (these are both investments designed to track a stock market index in a simple and cheap way – see glossary), not crazy tech firms.[46] "We're on a moving train," Eric Liu of Vanda Research, a group which tracks investor behaviour, told the *Financial Times* in March 2021. "In the past year we've yet to see a single major thematic move that has not been sponsored by retail." EToro is on the same page. "We believe that this growth is not just driven by Covid-19 but by a confluence of circumstances – the acceleration of digital technologies, commission-free stock investing and low interest rates – pushing retail participation in the capital markets. We believe that this trend is here to stay."[47]

There are other factors at play here too. The FCA

report on the high risks being taken by new investors also noted something important – possibly the most important thing of all. New investors said they enjoy the "status" that comes with a sense of ownership in the companies they invest in. That's the bit we need to capture – a sense of ownership. Almost all of us own shares and a lot of us feel pleased with that ownership. I think Mrs T would be pleased. However, she would not be ecstatic. Why? Because, while we think we want to be actively engaged with the companies we own tiny bits of via those shares, the vast majority of us aren't. And in most cases we can't be. It's all very well being proud of ownership, but what's the point of it if you haven't got the rights that come with it? In the next chapter we will look at where those rights have gone and why it matters.

3

IF YOU ARE THE OWNER, WHY DON'T YOU FEEL LIKE IT?

If most people in most developed democracies own shares, and most people know they own shares, it seems as if shareholder capitalism should be most people's system of choice. Everyone with a share gets a say, everyone makes money, everyone supports the system. We learn to understand what big companies can do – and what they can't do. We use our votes to let them know what we want them to do (remember that, in theory, the one-share one-vote system makes the stock market a democrat's dream) and we then support them in that. We act like owners and we feel like owners. Sounds great, doesn't it? Sadly, it hasn't worked out quite like that. Mostly, we don't feel like owners. That's something you can see reflected in the way we feel about the corporate system – we don't really feel good about it.

In a 2018 Gallup poll in which respondents were asked

if they were happy with the "size and influence of major corporations" in the US, 58% said no. The idea that our current form of capitalism isn't good enough is oddly popular: surveys regularly show 40–50% of Americans being quite keen on socialism,[48] and that 50% reckon that the economic system needs either complete or major reform.[49] The numbers in the UK and France are much the same (the Germans are even more negative – 70% want major change).[50]

This is not a mindset helped by the world of literature and film. Modern popular writers all seem to work within the same rigid mindset of good and bad, with evil multinational companies – there is no such thing as a well-meaning multinational in literature so far as I know – taking over from coal mines as top villains. I give you John Grisham (*The Runaway Jury*) and Michael Crichton (the *Jurassic Park* crisis is all the fault of a greedy billionaire and his company InGen). The rotten-to-the-core multinational is a constant theme in comic books too. Batman's Wayne Corporation is a force for good (it finances all Batman's gear) but what of Lex Corp, Oscorp and Hammer Industries? I'm slightly outside my area of competence here, but I don't think there's a goody among them.

Would we like big companies more if we felt we had some influence over them? Possibly. It's worth noting that, in the main, the closer we get to companies the more we like them. However, this isn't just about how we feel. It

45

is also about how company management feels: if our big companies felt that real owners, ordinary people, had influence over them, would they behave differently? I suspect they would.

So what's gone wrong here? The starting point to figuring this out is to think about what it actually means to own something. This is not as straightforward as you might think. Take, for example, a bit of land in Scotland. You can buy it. You can own it in law. But under Scotland's right-to-roam laws, you cannot prevent anyone else from walking on it. I like this – you could argue that it goes too far, that it steals privacy from landowners, but it mostly works and it's nice to be able to go wherever you please in Scotland. No barbed wire there. That said, if you don't have exclusive use of something, your ownership has obviously been diluted. Your ownership of the land is very different from, say, your ownership of this book.

It's complicated. In his 1961 essay on the subject, A.M. Honoré[51] had a go at making a list of criteria that might define ownership. There are 11. And the more of them you can say you meet, the stronger your claim to owning something. They include principles such as the right to possess the thing; the right to use it; the right to manage it; the right to receive the income or other benefit from it; the right to use the capital it represents (to destroy it or transfer it); the right to own it indefinitely if you choose to do so;

and the ability to leave it to heirs on your death. Look at that list and you might begin to wonder if you really own the shares you hold. You can't manage the company. You only get the dividends the firm's managers say you can have. You can't demand your share of the corporate assets from the managers (you can sell your shares but you can't exactly ring up and say you want your share of all the computers in the head office cashed in). As John Kay pointed out in the *Financial Times* in 2015, you also don't really have the right of possession or right of use of your part of the company.[52] If you wander along to Marks & Spencer or Walmart to spend the night kipping in the furniture section, you will "more likely than not be turned away". Overall, Kay reckons that "of 11 tests of owner-ship Mr Honoré put forward, the relationship between a company and its shareholders satisfies only two, and these rather minor. Three are satisfied in part; six are not met at all". Hmmm.

Who does have ownership? Look down the list again and you might think the answer is top management – holding as they do some of the rights of use of company assets and management. During 2020/21, the use of company-owned private jets for holiday trips soared. But it wasn't you or me who decided it would be neat to nip to the Bahamas for a couple of days, pandemic or no pandemic. It was top-ranking executives. Who owns the jet? Them? Or us? The truth is that the bigger and more complicated a company is and the more diverse its set of shareholders becomes, the more likely it is that the effective owners end up being the CEO and the rest of the board. Formal ownership may not rest with them but control certainly does. This is "managerial capitalism",[53] one in which economies are effectively controlled by large bureaucratic organisations run by lots of smartly dressed and highly paid managers, all hoping to end up with a corner office and a key to the executive loos. You could argue that this is the kind of capitalism that has been on the go in much of the West for most of the last 70 years; you could also argue that it is very far from ideal.

But what about the votes? If each share comes with a vote, shouldn't we at least have a say in who gets to be the CEO? Doesn't that represent ownership? Only if we are able to use those votes and do actually use them. And here we come to the nub of the problem. Mostly we can't. And when we can, we don't. It's all about the way we hold our shares. The share certificates we used to have entitled us to our dividends and gave us our vote. They also allowed us to receive communications (the annual report, for example) from the company. We don't have those certificates any more. Instead, those of us who buy and hold individual shares almost always do so via an investing platform. In the US, the big names are TD Ameritrade, Fidelity, Charles Schwab and E-Trade. In the UK, the big ones are Hargreaves Lansdown, Interactive Investor and AJ Bell. They're all perfectly good companies. But they all hold your shares in their accounts: you might be the beneficial owner, but they are the technical owners, so the votes rest with them. You can apply for your voting rights. But, while it is automatic at some forward-thinking firms, it isn't usually. Instead, it requires some form filling. The result? Most of us either don't know we have votes or, if we do, we are too admin-phobic or apathetic to use them – and as the companies themselves have no idea who we are (our holdings appear on their share-holder lists as "belonging to our platform"), they can't contact us to encourage us to get involved even if they want to.

UK investing platforms represent about £210bn of shareholder assets (as of March 2020). Those assets come with a lot of votes, votes that just aren't used. Interactive Investor offers a voting service to its clients at no extra charge (as all platforms should). In 2020, only a quarter of those who used the platform had signed up to use their votes. Worse, only 8% of all customers actually voted on anything at all. Overall, notes Schroder's Duncan Lamont, individual investors now end up voting on less than 30% of the shares they own. The private investor pressure group ShareAction has noticed this fall-off in obvious interest. AGMs, they say, have become increasingly quiet – individual investors aren't engaging or asking questions as they used to back in the day when they had a direct connection to the companies they held shares in. And this is key. Those votes could be used to express views on everything from the environmental conduct of a company to the extent to which it overpays its executives – to say nothing of protecting your rights by stopping it from issuing new shares to institutions but not to private shareholders, something that can dilute your ownership (and of course the value of your shares).

This is only the beginning of the problem. The next (and bigger) part of it is this: few of us any longer hold individual shares that we could, theoretically at least, use to vote on corporate policy. The proportion of shares held by individuals in the UK has continued to fall. From 66% in 1957,[54] it dropped to 47% in 1969. By 1994, it was only 20.3%.[55] It's now down to about 13%.[56] The numbers are similar across most markets – in Japan in the 1950s, ordinary investors owned 69% of the shares available directly. Now that number is 18%. Sure, we own equities. But we own them inside funds – we give our money to fund management companies, they pool it with lots of other people's money and invest it in one big lump. As the percentage owned by individuals has fallen, so that held by the big institutions has risen. In 1960, big institutions in the US owned around a third of the shares on Wall Street. By 1980, it was 60%. Now it is more like 80%.[57] In 1957, the combination of pension funds, insurance companies and investment funds owned a mere 18% of the shares in issue in the UK. That has steadily risen – to 60% in 1994 and up to 75% now.[58, 59] Not all of these institutions are UK based, of course – over 50% of UK shares are held by investors from the rest of the world in some form or another.

The fact remains that we don't directly control much of the game any more. Fund managers do. And they control a little more every year: global assets under management have risen from around $35tn at the start of the millennium to over $100tn now. Forty-one per cent of all equities globally are owned by institutions.[60] This makes sense. Investing is hard. It takes time and energy. Contracting it out to professionals is simple – particularly if you have barely even clocked the happy news that you have been auto-enrolled into a pension savings scheme (as you may have been in the UK, New Zealand, Canada, Chile, Germany, the US and Poland). This trend is also not likely to reverse any time soon. BlackRock recently received approval to start a wealth management business in China, for example.

The other thing to note is that when I say big in regard to fund managers, I mean very very big. This is an industry increasingly dominated by its own giants. In the US, the three largest asset management firms, BlackRock, Vanguard and State Street, together manage around $20tn of assets. That is one third of all the assets managed worldwide. It also means they control 80% of all the assets under management in the US. Hello, oligopoly. These US giants have long since landed in the UK too: BlackRock is now the largest asset manager in the UK. This represents real (and scary) change. Even 30 years ago, it would have been unusual for any one firm to hold more than 1% of the shares in a big organisation. Today in the US, one of the Big 3 is the top shareholder in 495 of the companies in the S&P 500 (this is an index that lists 500 of the biggest companies in the US).[61] All in all, they control what the pressure group Common Wealth calls (quite rightly) a "staggering" 20% of the average company in the index.[62] If things keep going in the same direction that number could soon be 40%. Given the general lack of interest about voting among other holders, in terms of voting rights that's more than enough clout to demand that a company does pretty much anything the Big 3 fancy (and they fancy a lot of stuff).

This is not only going on in the US. Take the UK as a rising example. The share of the average FTSE 100 company held by the top 10 investors (all institutions) rose from 36% in 2011 to 40% in 2020. That doesn't sound like much of a shift. But look inside and you see US managers growing their stakes significantly: the Big 3 held an average of 7% of the average FTSE 100 firm 10 years ago. Now it is 12%. Today, BlackRock and Vanguard control over 10% of more than two thirds of the 100 largest listed UK companies. BlackRock is the number one shareholder in 41 of those firms. Vanguard is top 10 shareholder in 98 of them. However you interpret the numbers, around a third of the invested capital in the world is run by 100 asset managers.[63]

Much of the money this lot run is what the industry refers to as passive – as opposed to active. Active fund management is the old-fashioned kind. We pay someone we think is tip-top at fund management to spend many fruitful hours fiddling around with figures to choose the best possible stocks to make us the most amount of money. Passive is the newer kind – in which we accept that most fund managers are rubbish and just ask them to ask a computer to choose a representative selection of shares in a market and hold them indefinitely – only buying or selling if the make-up of the index itself changes. That way we should make the same return as the market as a whole. The key point here is that the fund manager doesn't make decisions about what to buy or sell. He just holds the lot and hopes for the best – the best in this context being to track the returns from the index itself. We don't mind getting average returns – we just want to avoid overpaying someone to make us less-than-average returns. In the US, more money is now run passively for us by the big fund managers than is run actively.

In some ways this is brilliant – the cheap, simple nature of these funds has been one of the things that has pulled so many new people into equity investing in the last decade. But in other ways it isn't so good: it has made the big managers almost unimaginably powerful. They may hold all these shares on our behalf – but they are still the ones controlling the votes and hence, to a large degree, the companies. The person who most affects the behaviour of the big companies that we use to run every corner of our lives? Probably the CEO of BlackRock.

All this means that there is a huge dislocation between who we like to think is the end owner of shares (us) and who has the power to manage them and vote (fund managers). We might get our dividends and our capital gains, but things are a little blurred around the other rights that are supposed to come with share ownership – the right to participate at AGMs, to file resolutions and to vote on those resolutions, for example. The fund managers keep those. That in turn makes a difference (or could make a difference) to how big companies, and even economies, are run.

There is a view that none of this much matters. That we shouldn't worry about who effectively controls the shares, just about whether those who do are good stewards of our capital or not. Institutional investors use a high percentage of their votes.[64] They also have the time and the energy to work to understand the issues and are able to use the votes of so many shares at once that they can really influence outcomes. Viewed in this way, it makes sense to let them have the power. The long-term nature of institutional holdings also means that they provide permanent and stable capital: a good thing if they can then use the votes attached to this capital to act as agents of positive change too. Cyrus Taraporevala, president and CEO of State Street Global Advisors, makes the case for passive investing being even better than active in this context.[65] The great thing about passive investors, he says, is that they can't divest – they can't sell shares and they can't "choose the shares in which they invest". That means that at a time when any other investors are taking a short-term approach, they provide a "healthy and necessary counterweight". If individual investors can't, won't or don't want to vote, if the asset managers are good stewards, if they are voting as we want them to and if they are getting results from doing so, it makes sense to be absolutely fine with power shifting from company managers to asset managers. Pleased even. Getting hung up on the idea of ownership is silly in a world as complicated and as in need of expert supervision as ours. We should give it up. Goodbye, managerial capitalism. Hello, asset manager capitalism (or middleman capitalism).

You will note the word "if" doing an awful lot of heavy lifting there. First, it isn't clear that ordinary investors don't want to vote. All we know at the moment is that it is hard for us to vote – and that lots of us don't know we can vote. However, there are hints that the new generation of investors would very much like to use their influence – they tell every survey they come across that they are keen to invest in a way that aligns their money with their values, for example. Second, it isn't remotely clear that the big fund managers are good stewards, that they are getting results, or indeed that they are doing the things we want them to do. I'd argue that if they'd been doing what they are supposed to do – i.e. keeping an eye on long-term corporate sustainability – they might have had words with the big banks in the early 2000s and perhaps helped us avoid the worst of the Great Financial Crisis. They did not. They might also have taken action earlier on some other big issues that individual investors really care about. If they ever asked us what we thought, would the average CEO now earn well over 200 times the average worker in the US?[66] And if every asset manager really cared that much about all these issues, would the proxy advisory industry (an entire industry made up of firms that give voting recommendations to fund managers so they don't have to bother with the thinking themselves) even exist?[67]

For the last few decades, we've put our futures in other people's hands. We've given our money to fund managers and asked them to use it to make as much money for us as they can. We've trusted them to do what is in our interests (for a substantial fee). Along the way, we have asked them to also take on the stewardship role that comes with ownership – to act as owners for us. We disempowered ourselves – offering our votes to them. It isn't working. Asset management capitalism might sound good. But in no way is it good enough.

4

WHERE HAVE ALL
THE COMPANIES GONE?

If a crucial part of making shareholder capitalism work is ensuring that shareholder democracy plays a major role in it, it is obviously important that we have access to the ownership of as many companies as possible. But here there is a problem. The number of companies listed on global stock exchanges has been falling for years. At the end of September 2021, 2,004 companies were trading on the London Stock Exchange, down from 2,428 in 2000.[68] In 2019, just 36 companies floated initial public offerings (IPOs) in the UK – the smallest number for a decade. Overall, the number of companies listed in the UK has fallen by 50% in the last 45 years. It is a similar story in the US. There were 7,428 companies listed in the US in 1997 but by 2019 that number had dropped to 4,400 – partly as a result of a near 50% fall in new listings over the period.[69]

The home of modern shareholder capitalism could technically claim fewer listed companies than communist China.

A paper by Alexander Ljungqvist, Lars Persson and
Joacim Tåg[70] notes that it isn't just about companies not
listing. It is also about them delisting – being bought out in
their entirety by private firms and removed from the public
market. The firms listed are also getting older: the average
age of a US-listed firm has been rising for three decades.[71]
It is now 30 years. That's twice the figure of the days of
the dotcom craze. This is bad news for all sorts of reasons.
As Duncan Lamont points out, "public equity markets
represent the cheapest and most accessible way savers can
participate in the growth of the corporate sector". If they
are allowed to wither, ordinary investors miss out. That's
particularly the case if it is the fastest-growth companies
that aren't listing. Over time, if the best companies don't
list or end up leaving the stock market, returns from public
markets are likely to fall. Imagine you had invested $10,000
in Amazon in 1997 (or maybe don't – thinking of lost
opportunities can be depressing!). If you had, you'd have
$12m now. Amazon is an outlier, of course – you don't
get that kind of growth often. But small-growth companies
come with potential for extreme gain, and if they don't list
on the stock exchange, ordinary people have less access to
that potential gain than perhaps they should. There are
obviously implications here for wealth inequality (if too
much growth accrues in too few private hands) and hence

for public acceptance of capitalism; inequality is one of the things about it that people most object to.

Finally, of course, there is our topic – shareholder democracy. If companies aren't listing, we can't own them in such a way as to exercise any control over them. If we get to the point where ordinary people own too few shares in too few listed companies to feel invested in the corporate world or to care whether the government is friendly to business, politics itself will change. If companies aren't listed, we can't have a visible and comprehensible stake in them. Private companies are also not as visible or accountable as listed ones. And that has implications for the way in which we view the corporate sector. We don't often use words such as "shadowy" or "secretive" about listed companies – but think of a big private company and you'll find you almost automatically pop one of those words in front of it. Public ownership forces transparency on companies – which is surely a good thing.

A 2008 study by Prof Ljungqvist and his colleagues[72] even suggests that fewer listed stocks can lead to more anti-business governments. If you can see rising taxes on, say, payrolls or corporate profits cutting your dividend income year after year, you are likely to object. But if you don't get that you have a clear stake in the system, you might see no problem in rising regulation and a growing tax burden on business, for example. After all, business is "someone else" and someone else is always the person who should be paying the taxes. Once this process is under way – i.e. a government starts to become more anti-business – it is hard to reverse it. The result? Falling investment by businesses in the economy, a shrinking in the size of the overall pie and long-term losses for everyone. No good news here.

So what's going on? There are downsides to being listed: tedious meetings with analysts, stroppy retirees who attend AGMs, interference from fund managers trying to tick boxes proving good governance and environmental virtue, and relentless regulation and transparency requirements. As John Kay points out,[73] while corporations have always reported information to their members (even Victorian company law had them filing documents on a public register), those obligations have been so extended that all listed companies must now make available to everyone any information they have provided to anyone about their business. The idea here is that no one should have an information advantage – meaning less risk of insider dealing and a fairer market. But it also leads to trouble – it's too much work. The regulatory and disclosure requirements are now so onerous that all too many founders simply can't be bothered. Anyone in any doubt need only look at a modern company report – the average one contains 50,000 (mostly boring) words. These reports go almost entirely unread but are crammed with pages and pages of detailed information it takes companies (and their boards) far too much time to produce. There is a reason why almost half of the remaining listings in the UK market are on the Alternative Investment Market (AIM), a secondary market set up in 1995 that still allows companies to be public, but which comes with less arduous listing and disclosure rules. Add in the odds that more regulation demanding disclosure and action on diversity, climate and other issues is coming, and never listing at all or delisting might soon look even more attractive than it does now.

However, the matter of regulatory cost (and admin hell) is only part of the story: the fall in new listings was under way long before the most exacting regulations kicked in (in the early 2000s in the US).[74] There's also the matter of reputation. Public scrutiny of executives has increased fast too. It's hard to get away with anything – particularly if it is something social media doesn't like. Being the CEO or the founder of a listed company being brought to market used to bring a huge amount of status with it. These days, however good your intentions might be, it just means you are an easy target for a social media kicking – be it about your pay, your attitude to your workers, the value of your products or just the places you choose to go on holiday. You might get paid well (maybe too well) for the pleasure. But the fact remains that it's just not as easy, low cost or indeed as fun as it used to be to run or sit on the board of a listed company.

It's also the case that founders no longer have to go to the listed markets to get the money they need to expand.

Back to Amazon. When Jeff Bezos took his online retailer public in 1997, the company was three years old. He needed $50m, and at the time the public markets were the only place to get it – as would have been the case in any similar situation over the previous 100-odd years. Most of us have gained as a result of the listing (if you have a pension I can pretty much guarantee that one of the holdings in it is Amazon). By 2020, times had changed. Another e-commerce firm, the Hut Group, announced plans to list in the UK. But unlike Amazon, the company was already mature – 14 years old, with its major growth period (probably) behind it. It wasn't listing because its founders needed money to grow; it was listing because those who already owned the shares (mostly its original private equity backers) wanted to sell them and pocket a pile of cash.

These two listings tell the story of the past 20 years. According to a report from Morgan Stanley, companies have raised more money in private markets than public in the US every year since 2009 – Twitter raised $800m privately before listing in 2013, for example.[75] Companies are listing far less frequently and far later – often after their growth years have been financed by private equity. The average age of a 1990s firm at listing in the US was eight. Now it's 11. The likes of Uber and Airbnb are 3–4 years older than the typical firm opting for an IPO even 20 years ago. They haven't needed public markets for the very simple reason that private equity has been shovelling cash at them hand over fist. By 2018, private equity was providing five times more capital to companies than listings were. And by the end of the same year, there were more US companies owned by private equity than there were listed companies.[76] Between 2000 and 2018, as US listed firms fell in number from 7,000 to under 5,000, that of private-equity-backed firms[77] rose from 2,000 to close to 8,000.

This shift is partly down to private equity being where the easy money is. It is fuelled by debt – which, thanks to regular falls in interest rates, has been cheap and getting cheaper for 30 years. But it's also about the way in which big institutional investors want to invest. If you run a pension fund you are likely to be fretting about the yawning gap between the assets you hold in your fund and the amount you have technically guaranteed to pay out to your pensioners in the future. In the US, unfunded pension liabilities could run as high as $6tn (i.e. there's a $6tn difference between what they have and what they need). In the UK, the Pension Protection Fund notes a total deficit for defined benefit pension schemes of £200bn (that's a £200bn gap between what they have and what they need). There are three things managers can do about these horrors. They can pay less out to beneficiaries (no one is keen on this); pay more into the plan (the companies who would have to do the paying in on behalf of their employees and retirees don't like this); or finally, try and up the return on the assets they do have. Everyone likes this last option, but it is not as easy as it was. Just look at the history of the $350bn held by the California Public Employees' Retirement System (CalPERS). Until the early 1990s, you could get a high and safe return to build up your assets by just buying government bonds; in 1992 you got 7.75% interest – and your money back too. That was enough to beat inflation with a bit left over. All good – and enough to keep the show on the road. But by 2021 everything had changed: as interest rates have fallen so have the yields on offer on bonds[78] – US bonds were suddenly getting you not 7% but a mere 1.4%. Not nearly enough.

You see the problem. CalPERS began to feel it had no choice but to leave the safety of the bond market to look for higher returns wherever it could. That might have once meant putting more money in listed equity. It doesn't any more: giant US investment company GMO forecasts small falls in US equities over the next seven years, thanks to current levels of valuation.[79] With US equities in decline, managers are driven to seek out private equity in an attempt to bag the best returns early. The result: private equity money piles are at record highs. And, while the long term might of course show all this to be no more than a debt-driven fad (one that will collapse as interest rates rise), for now at least there is more coming. Nearly half of institutional investors recently surveyed by BlackRock said they were looking for more private equity. There's a silly amount of money knocking about, and that makes it easier for companies – particularly those with charismatic founders – to raise money outside the listed market. It also makes it easy for private equity companies to buy out already listed companies and take them private. Add it all up and private equity has become a great public-market-destroying machine.

You might say this doesn't matter: if the fund managers we invest with are the main investors in private equity, we are getting access to the same companies and same growth we would anyway. What difference does it make, particularly if private equity manages the companies well and makes good returns? After all, pension funds (and individuals) can buy private equity companies and get a piece of the action that way. I'd say there are two problems with that. First, double fees. The fund managers pay the private equity managers. We pay the fund managers and so end up on the hook for both sets of fees. And second, it means we have no say at all – no vote. Private equity people will tell you the great joy of what they do is that it allows them to own companies outright and run them in the way they like. There is no room for opinion from the likes of you and me in that story. That's a good thing for them but not necessarily for us. Good capitalism is transparent capitalism – and the private equity industry is very far from transparent.

You might also say that while I could be right, there is nothing to be done about this. Times have changed and that's that. John Kay is particularly interesting on this point. He believes that a large percentage of prominent companies just don't need as much capital as they might have done in decades past – and what they do need, they can get privately. The 20th-century corporations that we still think of when we think of listed companies required a lot of cash to get off the ground and to expand. The likes of General Motors needed to own endless plants, workers and materials (Ford even had its own rubber plantation in Brazil, where you can still find the now abandoned Fordlandia).[80] To raise the cash for all this stuff they needed shareholder support. Not any more.

Today's big companies don't need much start-up cash (Tesla aside). Amazon now owns a good amount of physical property and a fleet of cargo planes, but it leases warehouses. Apple leases stores. They don't own them. Google doesn't need either of those things – they might not even need offices (many employees are switching to permanent working from home post pandemic). Airbnb just needs a computer and some staff. No factory, no assembly line, no steel required. Why? Because it is only a technology platform – a middleman between the parties engaging in the real activity. The same goes for Deliveroo, which listed in London in early 2020. It doesn't make food and doesn't own the means by which food is delivered. It simply owns the technology platform that enables 100,000 cyclists and scooter owners to work with 115,000 restaurants in 12 countries. When it listed no one talked about the food; instead they called it "a global technology leader". Apple doesn't make a high percentage of its own products – it mostly designs things and contracts out their creation. It can double its business without adding a square foot of office space. These firms don't even need working capital as companies used to – you pay Apple before it pays the company that made your new phone in China. There are other types of infrastructure that new firms don't need in the way they used to either – think of the way we all hold our information in the cloud, for example. Expensive onsite company-owned servers not required.

Think, too, of access to customers. That used to be hard to gain. Today, points out Tom Slater of investment giant Baillie Gifford, a good company can use Amazon and eBay as a gateway to billions of potential customers instantly. You can get big these days – and stay private. Slater uses the example of Alibaba. When BG invested in it in 2012 at a valuation of $45bn, it was still a private company. In any other era, he says, a firm of that size would long since have been listed. The key thing is that this kind of firm doesn't need to raise capital in the way businesses used to. Instead, as was the case with the Hut Group, they only list to allow private shareholders an opportunity to sell to the not-so-lucky (those without access to private equity) once the days of real growth and value creation are over. We never see the big money.

This is irritating for one supremely obvious reason – it continues the trying trend of money accruing to those who already have it. But another infuriating aspect to it is that, if a company knows that once listed it is unlikely to have to raise money from investors (by issuing new shares) ever again, its managers might feel less inclined to have to please shareholders than otherwise. Take Google and Facebook, for example. We love their product (this book could not have been fact-checked without Google) but we wonder about how trustworthy they are, about what they do with our data, how they manage their tax affairs and about the influence their billionaire owners have over government. They don't feel like they are run for their shareholders – but for their founders and their managers. And even if they are listed, no one is putting forward resolutions about their behaviour at their AGMs.

But here's the question. Is this shift from the public markets inevitable? Kay thinks so. The modern corporation is, he says, defined by what it can do – what it can organise, rather than what it owns. Its value is in "problem-solving abilities founded on accumulated knowledge and experience – some codified, some tacit – and embedded in the social relationships that, taken as a whole, define the corporation". If capital isn't much needed, you can take a company from idea to multibillionaire creator without even glancing towards the public markets – or indeed offering those who invest there much of a crumb from your table. Listed companies belong, says Kay, to another era. They don't need us any more and we just have to get over it and shift our money into private equity funds run by managers who "build concentrated focused portfolios of companies they know well".[81] I'm not convinced this is completely right. We will always need expensive infrastructure. Think of the energy, transport and cement required for the green revolution, for example – and the strategic metals companies we need to build the mines to produce the materials we need to run the intangible economy. I also think it is entirely possible for policy to change to prevent him being right. In Chapter 8, we look at how tax policy and incentives might be revised to reverse the trend.

It is also worth noting that just as 2020/21 might have marked a turning point in the tide of ordinary investors (they're back), it may also have marked something of a turning point in the way companies look at markets. How? By reminding them that the core purpose of a public listing – access to equity finance from long-term shareholders – comes in very handy when you need cash fast. The numbers tell the story. Globally, listed companies raised $129.5bn in May 2020 alone – double the figure of May 2019. In the first half of 2020, US listed firms raised $125.6bn – the most in 30 years.[82] There has also been a very encouraging rise in the number of new companies coming to the market. The first quarter of 2021 was the strongest for global IPO activity in recent history, with 727 around the world (compared to 210 in the first quarter of 2020). Much of this has been in the US (58% in the first quarter of 2021) and much of it also reflected the listings of shell companies known as SPACs (special purpose acquisition vehicles),[83] but across the world real companies also listed, including Robinhood and The Honest Company in the US. There was major activity in the UK too – think Deliveroo, Darktrace, Moonpig and PensionBee.

The IPOs might not all be exactly what we would like to see – some have seen their major growth phase pass already (they were private equity backed during this phase) and lots were just speculative cash shells. But the numbers are still going in the right direction – and there are many ways in which we can help them to keep doing so. As with everything else, this is about incentives. It might make sense to cut back on policies, which, though ostensibly aimed at improving listed company governance, in reality add to the hassle of being public. It might make sense to allow something known as dual listings (offering two classes of shares, one with more voting rights attached to encourage founders to feel OK about listing – more on this in Chapter 8). It might also make sense to change the way private equity is taxed (far too generously at the moment). And social activists could rethink some of their efforts to make companies more political. If you had been thinking of listing, you could be put off by the public shaming of companies that paid dividends during the crisis. More radically, we could provide incentives – or even subsidies – for listing: what about a lower rate of corporation tax for smaller listed companies or perhaps a tax break on capital gains for founder-owners who list? There are options. But the priority must be to recognise that we lose a lot if we dismiss the idea that public markets should be the foundation of shareholder capitalism. There's a moment to catch here – as new investors meet new companies. We should try and catch it.

5

WHO'S ASKING AND WHO'S TELLING?

Now we know who has the power in all this, we need to ask how they are using it. If the major fund managers have the clout to boss the world's big (and not so big) companies around, what is it that they are bossing them to do? The answer to this question is bound up in a bigger one – what is the point of a company? In a seminal article in the *New York Times* in 1970, economist Milton Friedman argued that it was only to make profits for its shareholders. If this was done successfully the rest would follow – if you want to make long-term profits you need to make sure you incentivise employees and keep an eye on the resilience of your supply chain, for example. Focusing on profit makes the rest a given: a good business automatically drives good. Companies should make stuff or create a service within the appropriate regulatory boundaries, said Friedman; then sell it, and pay the proceeds to the providers of its capital. Aiming for anything else, he said, is to spend "someone else's money for a general social interest".[84] And why would you want to do that? This is shareholder capitalism.

The other part of the idea was that you need one firm metric to hold management to account. I wrote earlier about the risks inherent in managerial capitalism — i.e. when managers start acting as owners and then in ways we, the real owners, might not support (high pay for CEOs, low pay for workers and corporate jets for guess who…). To avoid that, we need to hold their feet to the fire with one set target that we know benefits all owners and pseudo-owners alike — money. Stakeholder capitalists disagree. They believe it is this focus on profit — and shareholder rights — above those of all others that has been responsible for the creation of most of the ills of modern society, from inequality to pollution and modern slavery. Their idea (and the idea so dominant today that it is almost unchallenged) is that the shareholder should only ever be a small part of the focus of a company. And that other stakeholders, including suppliers, customers, employees and the vague concept of the wider community, should be getting a look-in too.

There is much talk about environmental, social and governance (ESG) issues when it comes to investment at the moment. This is a more specific incarnation of the idea that companies should be judged not just on how they make money but on a variety of other metrics. Are they environmentally aware – and taking positive action as a result? Are they engaged with their communities and careful about the social implications of their behaviour? And are they well governed – in the sense of being compliant with all the regulations relevant to them and thoughtful about managing their risks? We hear of little else. But ESG is now something of a catch-all phrase, meaning pretty much whatever the speaker wants it to mean. Who should define it and how? And possibly more importantly, given that shareholder capitalism should surely also be shareholder democracy, who has ever asked us what we think about it – and indeed about the other big issues affecting the companies we think we own? Mostly no one.

So who is putting the pressure on? Who's doing the telling? The list is very long indeed. It starts with various government and supernational organisation groups (new legislation appears constantly). It moves on to non-industry pressure groups, fund management industry associations and of course individual fund management company "stewardship" departments. Let's name a few. In the UK, there is the Institutional Investors Group on Climate Change. Members include Legal & General, Aviva and the Church Commissioners (this lot manage the Church of England's considerable assets). They are currently after the banks with a view to making them go net zero well before 2050. How? By going for the banker's bonuses: they would like pay to be linked to progress on hitting emissions targets (targets they would presumably also like to set). This ask is part of a wider list of "investor expectations" rolled out by the group, telling banks how they are to play their "critical role" in bringing down global emissions (largely by not lending to oil and gas companies it seems).

In Australia, a new "Climate League 2030" is calling for companies to slash carbon emissions beyond government forecasts. In the US, the We Mean Business coalition is pushing for the same thing. Then there is Climate Action 100+, an affiliation of more than 300 investors, who control up to half of the world's capital, set up to try to persuade the 100 biggest carbon emitters in the world to change their ways. They do this via public letters (shaming), conversation with management and buying small numbers of shares in order to file shareholder resolutions (enabling them to present proposals for action at the AGM). There is also FollowThis, a group that tells us "green shareholders can save the world" and works to push big fund management groups to vote with them to get "Big Oil to go green". Australia has something similar in Market Forces.

These cause-specific groups are only the tip of the listen-to-us iceberg. In 2018, we saw the Embankment Project for

Inclusive Capitalism backed by a group of the world's biggest investors, including BlackRock, Vanguard and Amundi, the idea being to push companies to disclose information on everything ESG-related, from worker engagement to a firm's effect on the environment via a "standardised, material, and comparable set of metrics for the measurement of activities that create long-term value and that affect a broad range of stakeholders including customers, employees, suppliers, communities, and shareholders".[85] In 2019, the US Business Roundtable[86] decided to redefine the purpose of a corporation. A company, to their mind, is no longer only an entity that makes markets and sells something. Instead, it must have a "purpose" beyond that ("purpose" is another buzzword). It also has an obligation "to promote an economy that serves all Americans". It comes with five commitments – to customers, employees, suppliers, communities and shareholders – and promises that all signatories will "commit to lead their companies for the benefit of all stakeholders". You will note that shareholders come last in this list. This was soon followed by the Davos Manifesto 2020, which had another go at redefining the company. "The purpose of a company is to engage all its stakeholders in shared and sustained value creation… a company serves not only its shareholders but all its stakeholders – employees, customers, suppliers, local communities, and society at large." There is a list after this grand statement specifying how a company should treat five stakeholder groups. They are much the same as those listed by the Business Roundtable. Shareholders come last again – behind "society at large".

In 2018, The British Academy joined this bandwagon with Reforming Business for the 21st Century Framework.[87] Its website explains that corporations should have "clear public purposes". Here shareholders appear to fall even further down the list. Ownership, says the group, "in the context of purposeful corporations, is intimately associated with defining and delivering corporate purpose. It does not automatically attribute property rights to shareholders but recognises that different owners might be best suited to the achievement of different firms' purposes". That word soup might mean nothing at all – but I suspect that it means that the owner of any part of a company is whoever the groups want it to be. Hmm.

Next up are the UN Principles for Responsible Investment. The principles of this have been "developed for investors by investors", and the many signatories commit to agreeing that "we believe that environmental social and corporate governance (ESG) issues can affect the performance of investment portfolios" and that they will follow through by incorporating "ESG issues into investment analysis and decision-making processes".[88] Then there's the US Investor Stewardship Group (we should be playing do-goodery bingo here…). This one has created a "set of stewardship principles for institutional investors and corporate governance principles for US listed companies". It goes on rather ominously to announce that "listed companies should recognise that some of their largest investors now stand together behind these principles". Also worthy of mention in the UK is The Investment Association, which focuses a lot on pay and offers "red top" warnings about firms who aren't doing things quite as the association would like... All this before we start on the cause-specific activist and aggressive pressure groups (think Extinction Rebellion and so on). The world's charities have expectations too. Here's Kieron Boyle, head of the Guy's and St Thomas' Foundation. He thinks health "ought to be the key factor in investors' ESG (environmental, social and governance) decisions". Companies should have to disclose information on how their products affect consumer health, details on worker health, and community health ("the ways in which business activities shape the environment").

Add them all up and economist Dambisa Moyo reckons there are some 250 groups of substance pressurising businesses to do various good-sounding things.[89] I'd say at least. On a slightly different note, there are the proxy voting firms such as ISS and Glass Lewis. These are effectively advice firms – for the fund managers who either can't be bothered or who don't have the time or staff to figure out how to vote for themselves. Proxy voting groups give advice on hundreds of thousands of resolutions every year against a background of hugely complicated agendas. ISS says it covers 40,000 annual meetings a year in 117 countries, affecting more than eight million ballots. How's that for an unelected elite? Are they doing enough? Getting it right? Acting with nuance? Paying any attention to underlying shareholders? Just ticking millions of boxes? Who knows?

But these many hectoring alliances aside, the biggest and loudest voices come from individual fund managers themselves. They are the groups with the real power – in the form of the votes. Look at how they say they are investing and you can see the change over the last few years. In 2019, 39% of investing institutions said they did not implement specific ESG policies. In 2021, only 28% said the same.[90] So over 70% now claim they have ESG matters constantly on their minds. The number saying they integrate it into their processes was up from 19% to 48%. There are various ways to do this. Some use exclusionary strategies (they say they never buy companies doing what they consider to be bad stuff). Some say it is all about "active ownership" – buying companies that don't behave perfectly and encouraging them to do more of what the fund managers want. Some go for "impact investing" – only buying into companies that generate a positive ESG impact (however that is measured!) as well as the chance of a financial return. And some just go fully vague by claiming some kind of "best in class" style of picking shares for their portfolios.

You could easily argue that these definitions appear to

cover pretty much any activity (I'd agree), that they are in many cases so nebulous as to be meaningless and that everyone's criteria are completely different (one man's green dream is very often another's sin stock). You might also argue that this divergence of measurement makes a nonsense of the idea (held by 53% of institutional investors) that companies with better ESG records generate better investment returns. Perhaps those returns are not a function of corporate performance but of the demand for their shares generated in the scramble to offer an ESG portfolio?

But nonetheless, it is very clear that the mood music has changed. Here's Keith Skeoch, co-CEO of Standard Life Aberdeen (now abrdn) writing in the *Financial Times* in 2019. It is time, he said, to "recognise that the legitimacy of asset managers hinges on what they deliver for savers. It is an acknowledgement that these people have wider interests than just a financial return". He added that fund managers needed to "embed the environmental social and governance (ESG) factors that matter to savers at the heart of the investment process" and to "recognise that what is good for equity shareholders is not always in the interest of everyone who matters". We need, he said in the *Financial Times*,[91] to restore trust in business and to do that we need "companies to carefully consider what they do and to reconsider their place in society… corporate purpose must be more than a plaque in the reception area." Go Keith.

Skeoch is nothing on Larry Fink, CEO of BlackRock. Fink has been writing his annual letter (supposedly to the companies BlackRock invests in, but really designed to be read by us all) since 2012. In 2018, he started to come over all socially responsible. It was, he said, time for a new model of shareholder engagement. "To prosper over time every company must not only deliver financial performance but also show how it makes a positive contribution to society. Companies must benefit all their stakeholders including shareholders, employees, customers and the communities in which they operate." He had the grace to put shareholders at the top of his list, but you get the picture. Hmm, said one critic, "I didn't know Larry Fink had been made God."[92]

In his letter in 2019, Fink called on companies to fulfil a purpose (purpose again). Then in 2021, he went big on climate change. *Financial Times* columnist Gillian Tett describes Fink flying out to Alaska in late 2019 for a bit of "fly fishing, wine tasting and economic debate" with a friend.[93] On landing, he was horrified to find wild fires in Siberia meant the air was filled with smoke. This apparently caused his mind to "click" and suddenly see that "climate risk is investment risk". On to Larry's Letter 2021. In this one he announced that "climate transition marks a historic investment opportunity". There are "tectonic shifts" in markets ahead, he said, and all companies should become net-zero carbon emitters by 2050. He also said he would report the climate impact of all BlackRock funds and use shareholder votes to promote change (your votes, remember – for the change he wants).

Is Fink an unlikely hero, an opportunist (there is, as he rightly says, money aplenty to be made in the drive to zero carbon), a symbol of our age, or a catalyst for change? Tett thinks it's a mixture of the lot. Not everyone agrees. Hedge fund manager Chris Hohn says his letters are "full of greenwash". Still, Fink is getting louder. New inflows to BlackRock have been massive in the last few years – $527bn arrived in the 12 months to March 2021, Fink told the Bloomberg Green Summit, something he figured gave him a mandate for his views and his relentless expression of them. "I've been very loud at what I'm saying and I'm going to be loud again," he went on to say. And while he has neatly positioned himself as global hectorer in chief, he is very far from alone. Most big pension funds and managers are on the bandwagon – Goldman Sachs announced in 2021, for example, that they would not be taking any more US or European companies public unless they had at least one "diverse" director. And most also leave you in no doubt whatsoever that they are thinking about ESG issues. Remember the old (and I assume very out-of-fashion) joke about vegans. How do you know someone is a vegan? They'll tell you. How do you know a fund manager is interested in sustainability and stakeholder capitalism? They'll tell you. Oh yes they will, over and over again. In letters to the papers. In endless advertising campaigns. In interviews. At conferences. Anywhere you can fit the words stewardship and purpose into one sentence, you'll find a fund manager doing just that. No wonder 44% of CEOs surveyed by *Fortune* in 2019 felt they had to say that their company should "actively seek to solve major social problems as part of our business strategy". With that many censoring eyes looking over my shoulder, I'd say the same. By now, you might be beginning to wonder if buying shares should be classified as a charitable donation rather than an investment.

Maybe all this is OK. After all, there are lots of problems in the world. Maybe shareholder capitalism is at fault. And maybe allowing fund managers to use the almost unimaginable amount of power their voting blocs give them to sort it out is the answer. In many ways this makes sense, particularly if lots of the money is passively run – they only do well if everything does well, so those managers have an obvious interest in a better world long term. Fund managers have the ability, should they wish to use it (and increasingly it seems they do), to change the world in any way they want. The fund manager as enforcer and Larry Fink as God. In her book *Reimagining Capitalism*, Rebecca Henderson answers objections like this: "These owners are already exercising enormous power – in the service of pushing the firms in their portfolio in a race to the bottom. It's critically important that they make a deliberate decision to trigger a race to the top instead."[94] For her, the reimagined asset management sector is one that "takes its responsibilities to the world seriously and is willing to act on them". They should offer the "self-regulation" the private sector needs. You could also say that by giving your money to any one fund manager you are effectively voting for him as your steward and delegating all responsibility to him for a set period (much as you do when you vote in an election). Democracy in action. Sort of. You will have guessed that I don't buy any of this.

So what's the problem? Where to start! The first and most obvious point to make is that saying isn't doing. Repeat purpose over profit as many times as you like – but if you don't do something you are still nothing but an overpaid suit. And there is plenty of evidence of an epidemic of virtue signalling. There are so many different definitions of ESG, of sustainability and of general goodness that it's hard to know quite what each manager has in mind. There's also a veritable alphabet soup of letters and symbols attempting to define things, which somehow just make those things a little fuzzier along the way. In 2015, the UN launched its 17 sustainable development goals. Each has a logo, and each can, of course, be used as a marketing opportunity – stick a few on your fund literature, say you are investing in line with them and off you go. Overall, though, sustainable investing, ethical investing, ESG, green... whatever – they can mostly mean whatever you want them to mean. In 2019, Morningstar noted a "surge in funds rebranding as sustainable". In 2019, 360 new funds initially branded as sustainable hit the shelves in the EU. But another 250 just "repurposed from traditional to sustainable".[95] Some underwent a "complete makeover" but all too many others changed nothing about the funds. The name changes were "purely for marketing purposes". Run through the holdings in some labelled funds and you might be a tad surprised. Take the Legal & General MSCI World SRI Index fund (SRI is socially responsible investment). It holds Rio Tinto and alcohol supplier Diageo. In April 2021, one of the directors of the UK's Financial Conduct Authority told MPs that the regulator had seen "instances where what the fund says it is investing in does not really stack up with it being ESG". Who could possibly have guessed?

The second problem here is that if our many loud ESG devotees are in fact all hat, no cattle, all this guff might actually be a distraction from actually saving the world. Sceptics should read the words of the former sustainable investing CIO at BlackRock, Tariq Fancy (yes, Larry Fink's place – Fancy was there from January 2018 to September 2019). According to him the "multi-trillion arena of socially conscious investing is being presented as something it's not. In essence Wall Street is greenwashing the economic system and in the process creating a deadly distraction"[96] from the things that really need doing (stuff that would perhaps be better done by global government rather than companies). And as he says, "I should know, I was at the heart of it." He takes aim at the idea that ESG investing is a win-win (in that it'll make you more money while it saves the world), noting that "it works in a few instances and a few strategies". But it is mostly being blown out of all proportion. In truth, says Fancy, investors are being "duped": "sustainable investing boils down to little more than marketing hype, PR spin and disingenuous promises from the investment community." He gives this analogy: "Imagine the planet is a cancer patient, and climate change is the cancer. Wall Street is prescribing wheatgrass: a well-marketed, profitable idea that has no chance of curing or even slowing down the cancer. In this scenario, wheatgrass is the deadly distraction, misleading the public and delaying lifesaving measures like chemotherapy. But like giving false hope to unproven cures in the midst of a pandemic, the consequences of such irresponsibility are all too obvious. And motivation for why the industry continues to greenwash is all too obvious."

The third problem is that all this can also be a distraction from business success itself. *The Economist* ran an article in 2021 headlined "The Political CEO", which suggested that if we give CEOs the idea that they can step away from thinking of their shareholders to thinking of too many other things, they will (you don't get to be CEO without really loving power already).

But business and politics shouldn't mix too much. If there is stuff out there that we feel society wants – or indeed must have – should business have much of a say in it? Is it a good idea to ask fund managers and hence companies to pick up where the public sector leaves off – should they be the ones who fill the gaps where regulation is perceived as lacking? Should we really be relying on BlackRock to make sure that employment rights are up to scratch? That water is clean? That carbon concerns are addressed? Or is that overreach? Should all this not be the role of governments? Is this focus on non-financial targets by astonishingly powerful non-elected entities really democratic? I might be alone in finding the pronouncements from big cheeses in finance about how we should run the world a little scary, but I really shouldn't be. Look at the 2020 letter to shareholders from Jamie Dimon, CEO of JPMorgan Chase. It is 66 pages long[97] and gives us his thoughts on the purpose of companies, leadership and US public policy. This man doesn't just think he knows how to run a bank. No, he's got a total grip on how everyone else should deal with poverty (Dimon earned $31.6m in 2020 – I have some ideas for him), climate change, economic development and even racial inequality. We (the CEO "we" is similar to the royal "we" when used in this way) believe, he says, "that businesses' extraordinary capabilities are even more powerful when put to use in collaboration with governments' capabilities, particularly when seeking to solve our biggest economic and societal ills at the local level." Yikes. It's a full manifesto for a more progressive style of capitalism. One I am filing away in my very large file called "man who has made vast fortune calls for other people not to be allowed to make vast fortunes".

But at a micro level, how can all this grandstanding, virtue signalling and diversification of goals (we don't just want to make money, we want to micromanage the world) really be compatible with running an actual company (as opposed to sitting on top of an asset-gathering machine)? Maybe it isn't. Look, for example, at the shifts in the social justice environment. The kickback against shareholder primacy is opening the floodgates to pressure groups demanding that companies enter the culture wars – and that not only involves a lot of work but is fraught with danger too. There is now barely a brand left that hasn't run an inclusive campaign of some sort. See Coca-Cola's hosting of the "Together We Must" series of virtual dinners to discuss social justice topics, or Uber's anti-racist campaign ("If you tolerate racism, delete Uber"). In the UK, scores of companies supported footballer Marcus Rashford in his free school meals campaign and the Covid "we are all in this together" ads put out by many companies (mostly identical in format and message) were a classic of the genre (if you haven't already, look up the YouTube compilation). But it isn't just the planet and their clients that these newly stakeholder-focused companies feel they must help. Even before the pandemic, there was a new corporate paternalism at work. But now companies feel both an opportunity to tie in nervous employees with benefits and a responsibility for their physical and mental welfare. All forward-thinking firms have a wellness programme; most are at least considering hiring one of the new unconscious-bias training providers.

The modern company, then, has to save the planet (it "acts as a steward of the environmental and material universe for future generations", says the Davos Manifesto); enhance diversity; somehow guarantee the correctness of every link in its supply chain; eliminate the gender pay gap and child poverty; and, at least for now, safeguard its employees' mental, financial and physical health. A good company "fulfils human and societal aspirations". Consider supermarkets. In almost all of them you can now use a self-service checkout (assuming you can find a working one, of course). At Amazon Fresh stores you don't even have to do that – you just leave. On almost all levels this is fabulous. Quick, efficient and – surveys show – preferred by around half of supermarket shoppers. However, it comes with a downside. This "atomisation of the retail experience", as journalist Sathnam Sanghera calls it, is, say the naysayers, just another step on the road to loneliness and social isolation. Supermarkets should apparently be taking that into consideration when they decide on their checkout design.

But somewhere amid the paternalism and political

grandstanding, every company has to find the time and energy to sell stuff and make profits (in 2020 and 2021 with the added problem of rolling lockdowns). Much of what is being demanded of companies is good in its own right. But are we asking too much, particularly in such uncertain times? Let's not forget they are grappling with the fallout from the pandemic (although some, of course, have benefited hugely from it), a sharp rise in competitive pressures as every industry you can think of is disrupted by a new wave of rivals riding exciting technology waves; and the rolling-back of many decades of globalisation. Tariffs and physical barriers are rising, while the ability of workers to move around the world is increasingly constrained – meet the new world of protectionism. They've also got a fast-changing customer base (society is ageing fast, something the baby bust of 2020 did not help with), coupled with a skills shortage – in the West at least. The globalised world full of cheap capital, cheap workers and easy supply chains is gone. It's not an easy time to be running a global company. No wonder the exasperated CEO of Shopify found himself pointing out in mid 2021 that Shopify "is not the government. We cannot solve every societal problem here".

The genius of capitalism lies in specialisation and comparative advantage – it works best when we all focus on what we are good at. So expecting companies to have a purpose that goes beyond the obvious may be asking managers to juggle too many balls. If multiple layers of expectation are piled on top of a firm's core purpose, you end up burying it, or at least heavily distracting from it. Let's return to the supermarkets. As Sanghera says (unfashionably), social isolation is a "huge societal global problem that extends way beyond retail". It isn't a problem that retailers – whose job is to "sell things in the most convenient way possible" – can or should solve. Attempting to add a dollop of social care alongside selling oven chips really is something of a denial of comparative advantage.

There's also the constant risk of not all your managers or indeed your customers being on the same side of the culture wars. Remember when the Body Shop waded into the trans rights row in 2020, demanding that the brilliant J.K. Rowling read a book of their choice on the matter? A lot of women said they would never shop there again.[98] They may have turned out to want vegan bath bombs more than they wanted to punish the firm and returned as customers, but it wasn't a great day for the company, and you get the point. What if overreach inside stakeholder capitalism turns it into conflict capitalism?

Some reckon this is OK, possibly even the best way forward. Marketing professor Nirmalya Kumar thinks that these days, brands have to stand for something, particularly if they are targeting the young. In future, he says, the test of a great brand will always be whether they can answer yes to the question "Does anybody hate you?"[99] I hope that is not where we end up. Ultimately, surely the social welfare of individuals is more a matter for their families, friends, and for state-funded community services, than their employers. By the same token, the physical health of the population is a matter for public health services, while issues such as climate change are matters for governments to rule on. Companies pay taxes specifically (or are supposed to anyway) so that others do such stuff. Perhaps in the end the key aim of a business is to keep going. If the business doesn't keep going – and keep making money – none of the rest of the things that Dimon and Fink are mad for gets done at all.

One last potential problem. Ask too much from companies and might it not change the dynamics of investing? Might it, as Harvard Law School Professor, Jesse Fried, points out, make investors think twice before investing in a small, growing company? They lose if it fails (though this is a normal risk and one worth taking if you spread your risk around). And, if it goes public, its CEO might use its returns to serve "all manner of stakeholders with shareholder returns as an afterthought".[100] What's the point?

But all this aside, the real issue here is that no one asked you about this. There's a lot of telling, maybe even activism, going on. But it isn't coming from those of us who actually own the companies. It isn't your activism. It also isn't an activism that understands that stakeholder capitalism and shareholder capitalism are now often exactly the same thing. In 1970, almost no one owned shares. Now, in most developed countries, most people do. As mentioned earlier, we are shareholders but also customers, employees, suppliers and community members. So if you ask end shareholders (us) what we want, you will automatically hear from most stakeholders at the same time. We are the same people. No need to put stakeholders on the board. No need to agonise over the appropriate purpose for the company. No need to refer to any one of 250 advisory groups. How's that for efficient?

It is time to step back and think, not about what pressure groups and fund managers would like companies to do, but about what their actual end owners (us) want them to do. Do fund managers want what we want? Do they care what we want? Could it be that the view of an elite group of well-off fund managers might not be identical to that of the wider population of savers/voters? It might turn out that we all want the same thing. It also might not. And that is important.

6

WHAT WOULD BE DIFFERENT IF WE COULD USE OUR VOTES?

We know, we think, what we want. And on paper, at least, our wants align nicely with what our managers say they want (on our behalf). In surveys, we will always ask for the nice-sounding things: 68% of savers say they want their investments to consider the impact on people and the planet as well as to look for financial returns, while over 60% of fund selectors (the people who help pension funds choose which funds to buy) say they are going ESG because of "investor demand". Break it down into age groups and you will see apparent evidence of what you always hear – the young want their investments to do good more than the old. Seventy-four per cent of millennials and 68% of baby boomers say they want to make a "positive impact", while 83% of the former also say, perfectly reasonably, "I want my investments to match my personal values."[101] There's more granular data on expectations, too. A study from Aegon in 2020 reported that 77% of the people they interviewed said that climate change is an important risk to consider when investing; 59% said they cared about single-use plastic; 95% said they recycled; and 49% said that they considered the air miles of their purchases. In 2021, 63.9% also felt – and this is crucial – that investors should be asked to vote not just on ESG policy and targets but also on "key company developments with a significant ESG impact".[102] Look at the money flow and you see the same sentiments reflected.

Huge amounts of money have been flowing into ESG-biased funds: $152bn in 2020 alone. By the end of the year, there was $1.6tn under some kind of ESG management globally (these numbers begin to mean nothing after a while but trust me when I tell you this is real money).[103] That is, of course, nothing more than an indication of well-meaningness. The truth is that we mean all sorts of different things when we say we want to do good. Some of us care for nothing but the climate. Some of us mean we want to invest in renewable energy; some are happy with oil companies investing in renewable energy too. Some of us want to save the planet by going vegan. Some of us care about stalling the replacement of workers by machines – or at least finding a way to keep the workers working with the machines. Others care about holding back monopoly power or just want to make sure companies pay proper taxes so that governments can do all this stuff. Some want to invest in the companies that are trying the hardest ("best in class" investing) and some just want to know their manager is keeping an eye on things. Most of us have very little idea of what ESG actually means. And some of us don't give a hoot about any of this – we might want CEOs to ignore all the calls for diversity, social progressiveness and environmental initiatives and just get on with making stuff and making money. In fact, a fascinating study out in July 2021 suggested that an awful lot of people feel this way: the think tank Centre for Policy Studies found that 45% of people think that businesses should mostly avoid taking political positions or expressing political views, while 19% think they should do nothing but "make a profit so they can continue to create jobs for British workers".[104] Either way, if what we think we want is a little vague, what we get is even more so.

It's worth looking at the reasons why fund managers say they are implementing ESG: 57% say they are doing it to "align investment strategies with organisation values" and 35% to "influence corporate behaviour". Only 29% say it is about generating "higher risk-adjusted returns over the long term" and a mere 26% that it is to have a go at making the world better. There is improvement here (in 2014, 48% said it was purely a marketing measure). But it is still not what I want to lend my vote for. You'll note that none of the fund managers asked said they were just in it for the higher fees they can charge on ESG money, but that could easily be a factor too, possibly the biggest one, if my years of writing about the fund management industry have taught me anything. And what of the idea that they are influencing corporate behaviour in ways that we would like? In the *Financial Times* in May 2021, journalist Brooke Masters pointed out that fine words just aren't enough when it comes to key issues. Fund managers are endlessly going on about how important it is that high pay is aligned with performance and no end of other happy-sounding targets (19% of large public companies globally have some sort of environmental or social target in their executive pay plan).[105] Does that translate into anything meaningful? You know the answer to that. Of course it doesn't.

You will remember how companies across the world talked earnestly about their yearning to share our financial pain back in 2020. Sincere-looking CEOs telling us we were "all in this together"? There was lots of it about. By the end of June 2020, 502 US-listed companies had said they were going to make "adjustments" to their CEO pay to reflect the outbreak of public grandstanding.[106] Guess what has happened since. The median CEO package for Russell 3000 companies rose by 6% in 2020. At the largest businesses – those in the S&P 500 – median CEO pay (including bonuses and shares) hit $13.3m. That was the 11th straight annual increase. And, just for good measure, top executives spent more time on company private jets (for personal travel) than ever before. Because of the pandemic. That might just have been OK if the largesse had been spread around. But it wasn't. Median pay at S&P 500 companies dropped 17% on 2021. The ratio of CEO pay to employee pay? 227 times more. Heads they win, tails they win. Things were much better in the UK and in Europe – where total CEO compensation did fall. But you get the idea. Most pay plans are waved through by shareholders with 90% support. Earnest talk is one thing. Action is another.

If you are wondering how effective investing in an ESG-labelled fund really is, you might compare the shares held in one to those held in a standard fund. Often the top 10 holdings in the bigger funds are remarkably similar... Buy an ESG fund of any kind and mostly you will find you have a lot of technology companies, for example – technology isn't oil, mining or tobacco so has something of a head start in the ESG stakes. That might be OK. But there are also reasons, related to privacy, data use, social media addiction and tax, that will make many people think the big tech companies aren't any more straightforward as investments than alcohol companies. More food for thought (well, food for doubt really) comes in the form of the record of ESG-focused fund managers on shareholder resolutions in general. Those who say there is no point in private shareholders having their own power argue we won't use our votes if we have them. But do *they* use them? Not so much. ShareAction recently looked at this.[107] Overall, only six asset managers globally managed to vote on 95% or more of the resolutions they could have voted on. Five of them voted on fewer than 20%. BlackRock and Vanguard were both in that group of five. This, says ShareAction, is "a warning sign that these managers are failing to deliver on basic stewardship activity".

Here's a favourite story. In 2021, BlackRock joined a shareholders' protest against Procter & Gamble over the latter's palm oil supply chain. BlackRock said it felt there was room for P&G to improve. P&G then looked into various problems at one of the suppliers in question. And one of the biggest investors in that supplier? You guessed it. BlackRock.[108] ESG can be complicated. There's more. Just 15 out of 102 shareholder resolutions (the ones put by investors as opposed to by the companies themselves) passed in 2019/20. The votes on climate change make for especially interesting reading. Thirty-seven of the asset managers ShareAction looked at are members of the Climate Action 100+ group we saw in the last chapter. They vote on more climate resolutions than the average asset manager. But even here, five members voted on less than 50% of climate resolutions.[109] BlackRock supported just 6% of environmental proposals filed by shareholders globally in the year to June 2020.[110] Not all fund managers are useless at this stuff – Impax Asset Management reli- giously votes on everything, for example – but overall it still isn't good enough. And even if it were – even if all managers voted on everything, how would we know they were voting in a way that worked for us, and our vision of society and the future? However well they might or might not do the stewardship part of their job, the middleman – or agency – problem still exists. Whatever we say in surveys and however much fund managers say they are listening to what we say in those surveys, this isn't working.

So if we were to find a way to use our votes – the ones we have as direct holders of shares and that we should have as investors in funds that hold shares for us – what would change? The first and most important answer to that absolutely has to be "I don't know". That's the whole point of a democracy – everyone gets to vote and the outcome, while mostly OK, is uncertain. But I can take a few guesses. I suspect we'd call time on the pay merry-go-round. One of the things that drives ordinary shareholders mad once you get into it is the entitlement bias of company directors. Directors aren't necessarily entrepreneurs and in the main did not set up the firms they run – but nonetheless consistently find reason to use companies to make themselves long-term fortunes. If ordinary investors had got to use their votes over remuneration policy, would this problem ever have a) started and b) dragged on so long? It is worth noting that this is one of the many things that the fund managers holding our votes talk about a lot but do very little about. If you are a fund manager paid £500,000 or indeed at the top end £10m plus (Larry Fink's total compensation in 2020 came to just under $30m), how loudly are you going to complain about a CEO being paid £10m? And if you have been in your own job for 20 years despite mediocre performance (the norm for fund managers), how hard will you push to replace a not brilliant board of directors elsewhere?

You will hear a lot about aligning pay with progress and performance. That's fine. But whatever the justification for them, the underlying numbers are all too often obscene – how can it be right that being made CEO of a listed company (that you did not found) can make you enough money to transform the fortunes of your family for generations to come? The one that will stick in all UK investor minds will be the shocking case of Jeff Fairburn, one-time boss of Persimmon Homes and the man who became a textbook example of corporate governance failure, when, largely on the back of profits funded by the taxpayer-backed (and awful) UK Help to Buy scheme, he was given a bonus of £76m.[111] Yes, £76m. That's quite a transfer of wealth from shareholder to manager, isn't it? The asset managers let his badly designed bonus structure through the net. Would we have? As an aside, check your ESG fund and see if Persimmon is in it. The G stands for governance – is it possible to argue that, over the last decade or so, fund managers have really been monitoring this properly?

Still, while £76m might be an outlier even in this

context, big money deals are everywhere. What of the Pearson chief executive Andy Bird? In late 2020, he was given annual pay of up to £5.9m and a "golden hello" of £7m. Oh and £185,000 a year to help him rent an apartment in New York. Nice work if you can get it. Would we have let him get it? In spring 2021, mining company Glencore proposed a pay scheme for their new chief executive worth up to $10.4m a year. Twenty-five per cent of those who voted on this at the AGM voted against it. That's something. But what of the other 75%? Looks like they figured (largely on your behalf) that it was just fine. In 2018, BlackRock voted against just 11% of the top 100 pay awards in the US. Fidelity voted against 7%.[112]

Big pay-outs for no obvious reason have long been a problem – but the pandemic made the most egregious of them more obvious than usual. There is no shortage of executives who have made fortunes largely as a result of a stock market boom that has nothing to do with them, or as a result of their competitors being forcibly closed (if people buy more food in your supermarket because they aren't allowed to go to restaurants, should you get a big bonus?). Much of the pay problem can be laid at the door of long-term incentive plans for management. These are often not very long term, incentivise the wrong things and are almost always insanely complicated. I like to think that you and I would demand at the very least simplicity from them. I have some evidence for that thought: data in the

US shows that when it comes to "say on pay" resolutions, private shareholders are four times as likely to vote against high pay than institutional investors are.[113] Lower and properly long-term pay would be a good thing – particularly if we could all understand how the final number was calculated. The same goes for CEO pensions. In 2019, the average FTSE 100 employer contribution to staff pensions was around 10%. The average for chief executives? Twenty-five per cent.

There has been a little more focus on all this since the beginning of the pandemic. In May 2021, General Electric shareholders rejected a pay deal for CEO Larry Culp.[114] Quite right, you will say – it was so badly designed that he was in line for a potential pay-out of $230m. So it's good news that the asset management institutions finally grew a little backbone. The bad news? In the US these votes are non-binding; the company shook its collective head sadly and said it was "disappointed" and would continue to engage. They also said they would not be raising their dividend. Maddening stuff. There is, however, another solution for fund managers who really mean it on pay – they can vote against the directors responsible for giving out, or receiving, the silly money. Those votes are binding. There was a kerfuffle at the Rio Tinto meeting in 2021 about chief executive pay, for example, when 61% of investor votes went against it. Progress, you might think. You'd be wrong. If it represented real progress, the same investors would have voted against the head of the pay committee at Rio. They did not (the vote went 95% in his favour). Not progress. Just showboating. At an AGM for one of the boards I sit on, an elderly shareholder rose at one point to ask us to note that our (non-executive) chairman's pay for attending six meetings a year was more than his entire annual income. That focused our minds. I think of it still today at every remuneration committee meeting I attend. If only all remuneration committees did likewise.

Pay-related examples are endless. But there are all sorts of other trade-offs we might start to think about. Would we vote to trade profits for carbon reduction strategies that go beyond regulatory requirements? For higher wages for employees? For charitable giving? To pay more tax? After all, a few percentage points more in tax taken from each giant technology company and we could all stop bickering about what 1% here or there on income tax might or might not do. What about forced labour? We would surely all vote for supply chains to be clean. In 2020, it became clear that companies all over the world produced products that at some point relied on using Uighur Muslims as forced labour. I think we would all want to vote for our companies to step up their vigilance there. Might we also see a fall-off in short-termism? The best time frame you can usually get out of a fund manager for "long term" is five years (as long as they can underperform the market without being fired). But for most of us, long term is a lot longer than that.

Not only does no one pay us a bonus if we outperform the market (or gather lots of assets to manage and charge fees on) over a one- or two-year period, but most of our share ownership is inside our pensions. For the young that makes long term 40-odd years. And even for 50-year-olds, long term is 20 years – we might be dividing our portfolio up into a part we need in 10 years but there'll still be lots we shouldn't need for 25 years. What we are after here is a long-term income or a capital gain to convert into income for what we hope will be long retirements. Perhaps we'd forgo special dividends (where companies distribute excess profits in a one-off payment to shareholders) and even ordinary dividends for more money being invested in the business to keep it going in the long term. We don't just need money now – we need it later too. With that in mind, perhaps we might also vote against some of the mergers and takeovers fund managers like so much.

Let's look at some examples of what small shareholders might want to do. In 2021, some of McDonalds's' investors submitted a resolution asking the firm to fund a study into how much the use – or overuse – of antibiotics is costing public health. They supposed that as meat suppliers are some of the biggest users of antibiotics, it made sense for the fast-food firm to be onside with the study. After all, while the antibiotics might be good for the firm and shareholders in the short term (cheaper meat), in the long term antibiotic resistance might mean everyone pays the price. McDonald's wasn't keen on this. The firm said it had put its Vision for Antimicrobial Stewardship in place in 2017; it was working with suppliers to gather data on antibiotic use; and was also already working to end the use of any antibiotics that are specifically medically important to humans. All in all, it said creating the report would be a waste of money and time.

If you have a pension, odds are it holds some McDonald's shares. Given that, wouldn't you like to have had a say on this crucial topic? Would we have voted differently from the world's big institutions (the Big 3 US fund managers who own 18% of the shares)?[115] And what of animal welfare issues? We might be more concerned about these than perhaps institutional managers are. On the same theme – also in 2021, a People for the Ethical Treatment of Animals-backed shareholder resolution (PETA buys shares in companies it wants to encourage to change) at Lululemon Athletica asked shareholders if the company should stop using bird down in clothing. Those who backed it worried that the birds used for the down underwent inhumane treatment – they were crammed into confined spaces and ineffectively stunned at the slaughterhouse. The company management asked shareholders to reject the resolution on the basis that their policies were certified under the Responsible Down Standard and that they believed that "decisions about materials used should be made by design teams, not the board of directors or shareholders". The resolution was rejected. Go on to the website today and you can buy a jacket stuffed with grey goose down for £348. But if you had been able to vote, would an awful lot of geese have been saved an awful lot of suffering? When shareholder information group Tumelo (more on this in the next chapter – they are part of the solution) asked those who hold shares in Lululemon via funds how they would have voted, 55% said that they would have voted for the resolution (no more goose down).

Perhaps we will also make more careful decisions about the trade-off between do-goodery and making nice financial returns. I'd say the jury is very much out on this. First, common sense (and a huge amount of evidence) tells you that if you limit the universe in which you invest, you automatically cut the extent of your potential performance. Constrain a portfolio (with the idea of increasing its ESG score) and you constrain your returns. That's particularly true as ESG funds get more expensive (everyone wants them). The higher the price you pay, the lower your expected long-term returns are. The evidence that this is not the case is based mostly on the last decade (there was no critical mass of ESG-related investment before this), a period in which tech stocks, a mainstay of ESG-style portfolios, have wildly outperformed. That won't last. Look to the past and you can see the problem. A 2008 paper by Frank Fabozzi looked at returns from "sin stocks" in 21 countries from 1970 to 2007.[116] The sin stocks outperformed in all countries over the period. That does make sense. If everyone avoids the "bad" and piles into the "good", the former becomes cheap and the latter expensive. Future returns are everywhere and always a function of the price you pay when you buy. It's also true that "bad" companies can benefit from a lack of new competition. If you are doing well in renewable energy or, say, cyber security, you can be pretty damn sure that there are a good many clever competitors snapping at your heels. But who on earth would be able to raise money now to start a new cigarette firm or to explore for oil in someone's pristine seas? It may be true long term that virtue is its own reward.[117] But it isn't something I'd want my fund manager and his "ESG-is-a-win-win" crowd to bet on without checking with me first that in theory I was happy to take a financial hit to help the world achieve non-financial goals. There is some worry around this subject. The US Department of Labor has stipulated that pension funds must not place ESG requirements above financial returns when choosing investments. The idea here is to make sure that the funds actually provide "for the retirement security of American workers".

Here's one example of how that might happen. Divestment. If you consider yourself a good person, you won't hold shares in any companies involved in fossil fuels or mining. Their activities are dirty and environmentally unsound. You can't believe the planet is in trouble and also

109

invest in businesses involved in creating that trouble. End of. This is certainly the view held by the likes of Friends of the Earth.[118] But might, just might, there be another way of looking at this, one that is just a bit hard to hear over the cacophony of ostentatious virtue signalling? The first question to ask is exactly what divesting – selling shares in "bad" companies of this sort – achieves. I'd venture nothing good. When you sell the shares, someone else buys them and the business just carries on. The transition to cleaner energy is under way. But it's going to take several decades. In the meantime, we need traditional sources of energy. Shouting at oil doesn't change that. You could even call it, as a former UK pensions minister did, "reverse green-washing" – something which might make you look good but which does nothing to fix the real problem.[119] You can argue this even more forcefully when it comes to the mines. If you want to get rid of the combustion engine – and find me someone who will say they don't – you will need copper, as copper wire is one of the best ways to move electricity around. You will need mountains of rare-earth metals too, for the magnets in electric motors and lithium for batteries. A medium-sized electric car currently contains 2–3 times as much copper as a comparable conventional car. A single 3 MW wind turbine contains approximately 4.7 tons of copper.[120] Net zero might be a grubbier business than some like to think. What we want, then, is not no oil, no tin and no copper, but more carefully produced oil, tin and copper.

How do you get that? Not by making a show of flouncing off in a huff but by staying invested and encouraging better behaviour.

There's something else the divesting cheerleaders need to bear in mind. Selling shares might not make any difference to a business, but it makes a difference to who *owns* the business. If you make a big institutional holder who really cares about, say, the climate, sell to a private holder who really doesn't, what exactly have you achieved? Take that a little further and imagine Friends of the Earth persuading all UK funds to sell fossil fuel firms. Those sales push the share prices down and down again. They become cheap. Very cheap. But those who invest in listed companies are too media-aware to buy them back. The result? The companies are taken private by someone, maybe in the UK, maybe abroad, who doesn't care what Friends of the Earth thinks. Now not only are their assets held by someone who might be, as Total's chief executive puts it, less "mindful" than the original owners, but oil production continues just as before. Is that what we really want? And in particular, is it what you want when there is still plenty of money around in this sector and you have a pension to finance? You might feel differently from the average fund manager about these issues – and you might vote differently.

There's a similar dynamic in tobacco. In 2021, a group called Spring Mountain Investments (a company controlled by a man mostly referred to in the press as a "secretive billionaire investor") started to build stakes in British American Tobacco and Imperial Brands on the cheap. Will this group be a better owner than you? Will it use the dividends better than you would have? Questions worth asking. Put divestment aside and imagine your fund holds shares in a big oil company. To align themselves with their firm's vision, the fund manager votes for the oil company to cut dividends and use the cash to shift to investment in renewables. You might say, hmm, but we need the oil for the next 30 years and I need the income for the next 30 years. Perhaps all this is best left? This exemplifies what I mean when I say that what they want and what you want might well be different – even if surveys suggest otherwise. Specifics have outcomes that generalities don't flag.

However, as important as all the possible specific outcomes might be, the most far-reaching effect of using our votes and re-engaging with the corporate world is likely to be a new understanding of how it works and a rise in the level of trust we have in it. The 2020 Edelman Trust Barometer showed that 56% of people thought that capitalism did more harm than good and fewer than one in five people felt that the system was working for them. And while more people than not thought business was competent, fewer than half thought it was ethical. Asked in Gallup polls how they felt about the size and influence of major corporations, 73% of people said they were some-what or very dissatisfied. Asked if they had confidence in these big businesses, 45% said some, 33% very little and 3% none.[121] Not a huge vote of confidence, is it? Young adults in particular have been turning against the idea of capitalism: a 2019 poll in the US showed that, while 66% of them viewed it positively in 2010, a mere 49% do now (among the baby boomers the number is 68%).[122]

It is clear that a lot of this distrust and dissatisfaction is about distance. Small businesses remain popular and trusted by most people – 97% of respondents told a Gallup poll in 2019 that they had a "positive image" of them. There was also evidence that people had very high levels of trust in their employers during the pandemic. In a US-focused Axios/Ipsos poll, 72% said they had either "a great deal" or "a fair amount" of trust in their employer (34% said the same for the federal government). Might it be that the closer we get to a business and the more we understand it, barring actual bad behaviour, the more we understand its complications, conflicts and virtues? I also suspect that the more agency we have over a company – or feel we have, at least – the happier we will feel about its workings. As Gavin Oldham, the CEO of the Share Centre (now part of Interactive Investor), said a few years ago: "If shareholders don't feel they have any say over the companies they own, then they are likely to challenge the whole basis of the system." If they do, perhaps they won't.

It is also possible that levels of trust would rise. As author Michael O'Leary points out, the public tend to say they don't trust financial services or big business.[123] But ask them about corporate capitalism in action – the goods and services they get, the brands they like and the businesses they are close to and that changes. Look at attitudes in the UK to immigration. As soon as the Brexit vote result was announced, they softened remarkably. It turns out that fear of immigration was not about immigration itself but about not being able to control it (a fear with some basis – some five million EU citizens registered for settled status in the UK post Brexit, a good two million more than the government knew were in the country). Once it was established that power over the matter had shifted (to domestic authorities), tension eased immediately.[124]

If we all know we can vote, and if we all do vote, what happens when one of the world's frequent corporate scandals occurs? Do we blame fund managers and management, or do we look to ourselves? And is the latter better? I think so. Knowledge of ownership leads to engagement. The more we engage, the more we feel like owners. And, I suspect, the more we understand that we are all part of the same ecosystem, the better we will feel about democratic capitalism. If we could vote, if we knew we could vote and if we did vote, we could and probably would change the world – and save the system that has served us all so well along the way.

7

SOME PROGRESS

There is progress. We are slowly moving towards returning the rights of ownership to the real owners. First up is a renewed focus on finding easy ways for individual investors holding individual shares to properly use the rights that come with their ownership. In the UK, that impetus is partly coming from the investor platforms. This may be because it's a great marketing opportunity (we are making sure what's yours is yours etc); or because they are responding to lobbying from shareholder support groups (in the UK ShareSoc is brilliant at championing the rights of individual investors); or even because they share my passion for the rebuilding of shareholder democracy. It could also be all three. Either way, it's happening. The big platforms in the UK are all working to make it easier for shareholders to claim their rights – Interactive Investor is, for example, working to remove the bureaucratic blocks to this completely by opting all clients into their voting system automatically.

And it is not, by the way, as if people aren't voting at all. In the first quarter of 2021, 26% of over-65s were already signed up to use the Interactive Investor voting service. The 55–64 age group were also reasonably prepared to engage – 24% of them signed up. It's worse in the lower age groups – only 15% of those aged 18–34 were signed up. And it's true that it's a bit lacklustre if you look not just at who signed up but also at what percentage of accounts actually voted – only about 14% overall (although 21% of customers say they vote "at least sometimes"). On the plus side, that's up from 9% in 2020 – and has scope to go higher. Almost a third say they would be more likely to vote if they felt that their vote would affect the way the company was run. This is something of a chicken-and-egg situation: the more individual investors vote the more they can affect the way a company is run. In the US, the numbers are higher: between 2015 and 2017 retail investors cast around 30% of their votes.[125]

There's also been a silver lining to the pandemic as far as AGMs are concerned. I was a bit down on the idea of online AGMs at the start of the pandemic – they seemed to shut shareholders out more than let them in. But as they have been refined, they have begun to work out rather well – with more investors participating than when they had to turn up in person. Rather than destroying the AGM,

Covid turned out to have offered companies a fabulous chance to reimagine it.[126] This, along with the new surge of individual investors in all sorts of companies, is making those companies think harder about how to engage with small shareholders. That means special online events, podcasts, social media interaction and so on – all aimed at the likes of "us" not the likes of "them".

Take CarParts.com. It saw its shares rise substantially thanks to private investor interest in early 2021. Until then, its investor relations department mainly pandered to institutional investors. No more. In the spring, it planned a separate event for small investors. "We want to let them ask us anything," said the COO David Meniane to the *Wall Street Journal*. Investor relations advisers are all over this: it is time, they say, for companies to explain themselves in language individual investors understand, to take questions from them (regularly) and to ask them what they want from companies. There are also organisations popping up to facilitate communications between companies and smaller shareholders – in the US there is Say Technologies and in the UK, Investor Meet Company. The former allows all investors to pose questions to companies that have signed up and to "upvote" other people's questions. The most popular rise to the top, allowing companies to get a real handle on what their shareholders are thinking – and to make sure they answer the right questions at their AGMs. Tesla used the system to discuss their third-quarter earnings in 2020: the top questions were shared nearly half a million times. The Say Technologies website proclaims that "no shareholder is too small" to sign up and participate, that all shareholders should "stop throwing your vote in the garbage and start using Say to vote your shares". I also like an initiative from Marks & Spencer, a company that has long had a close relationship with its small shareholders. The company has had a shareholder panel since 2016: every year you can apply to sit on it and, if chosen, meet with senior management "on several occasions over the course of the year" to discuss all things M&S.[127] It works. As M&S says, "Our private shareholders are not only financially invested in M&S, they are some of our most loyal customers who care deeply about our business." And as one of their committee members says, "This has made me feel a lot better about M&S. Instead of whinging, I've had my say." That's what we want to hear.

This is all going in very much the right direction. But what of the real issue – the majority of voting rights that we have lost by inadvertently delegating them to the asset management industry? Most of the fund management industry still seems to think that it makes sense for us to leave the stewardship of the corporate world to them. After all, they're the experts. But a few voices of reason are appearing in the wilderness. The PRI (Principles for Responsible Investment), a United-Nations-supported international network of investors, has released a paper entitled "Understanding and Aligning with Beneficiaries' Sustainability Preferences".[128] There is, it says, a growing acknowledgement that investments should "reflect the values of their beneficiaries" and "increased realisation" that there are benefits to this. It makes sense, they say, because beneficiaries are increasingly aware (hooray!) that their investments affect them in non-financial ways – as "employees, consumers, community members and citizens" (I'm not sure what the difference is between the last two but we will go with it anyway).

For the PRI, a key benefit is that when people really understand how their savings interact with their everyday lives and the positive outcomes their savings facilitate, they may "be more inclined to contribute additional monies to their investments". Note that a 2020 survey found that 60% of New Zealanders said they would be motivated to save and invest more money "to make a positive difference to the environment and society". How's that for a win-win?

There is also a competitive element to this. If you can tell potential clients that you are listening to them, you can appeal to new groups of investors – those who want a voice and those who value sustainability. With this in mind, the PRI argues that managers should actually ask beneficiaries what they want via surveys, interviews, focus groups or forums of one kind or another. The results should not be binding (we aren't there yet) but they should be integrated into "decision making on investment allocation and stewardship including policy engagement". Finally, they should report back to beneficiaries on any action they have taken following these consultations "to encourage a virtuous circle of engagement". Sounds good, doesn't it? We could quibble with the binding bit but progress is progress.

Some regulatory shifts are also taking place. Small so far – but interesting nonetheless. The UK and Japanese Stewardship Codes ask signatories to consider beneficiary preferences and the European Securities and Markets Authority currently considers it good practice for investment firms to collect information on client ESG preferences. Regulators in the US are beginning to get it too.[129] Allison Herren Lee, a commissioner at the Securities and Exchange Commission, is keen to improve the transparency around how our shares are voted. In a great speech in 2021 ("Every Vote Counts"), she noted that, while nearly half of US households own a fund of some sort, they have no say at all over the voting policies of asset managers. That, she says, simply isn't good enough. "Our regulations have not kept up with this new landscape of institutional-investor-driven corporate governance." Indeed they have not. Her solutions? That retail investors need "more meaningful insight into how their money is voted" via a more transparent system than is in place at the moment. She is also open to exploring "the use of a permissioned blockchain to record beneficial ownership and execute votes".

Blockchain is the technology underpinning the crypto-currency craze. Herren Lee's suggestion would be a very useful way to shift it from being a facilitator of speculation to the foundations of a new age of shareholder democracy.[130] How? By cutting through the layers of intermediaries between the technical ownership of a share and its final beneficial owner (the person who gets the dividends and who should have the vote). It can be used to assign actual ownership and hence voting rights. Herren Lee says there is a lot of work to do in this area but her summing-up words should be music to all our ears: "It is important work because it gets to the heart of ensuring that our system of shareholder democracy works."

Good news, then. The tide is turning. But will we use our power if – when – we get it? When I wrote about shareholder democracy in the *Financial Times* a few years ago, most of the responses were pretty snotty. It doesn't work, they said – people don't care enough to use their votes. I don't buy that at all. Instead, the lack of engagement is due to a mixture of several issues. When it comes to individual shares, people often don't know they have ownership rights. And when they do, they don't know how to use them – or can't quite make themselves do the admin to use them. When Interactive Investor sent emails around reminding people they could register on the website to vote, a large number opened the email. The interest was there. But not very many actually registered – the admin was too much for them. Hence the company's decision to shift to asking people to opt out rather than in. It'll be interesting to see what happens now. When it comes to funds, the truth is that most people don't even know that their pension is a selection of funds held inside a tax-efficient wrapper. And, if they know they have funds, they often have no idea that inside them are shares in actual companies, let alone that those shares come with voting rights and give someone somewhere power.

This may change slowly. One reason to believe it will is the shift to an auto-enrolment-defined pension system in many countries that we discussed in Chapter 2. In the UK, it used to be the case that the average person had no need to engage with the asset management industry. You built up a pension over time with your company. On retirement it either automatically paid you a set sum every year for ever or you swapped the cash you had built up for an annuity – which also effectively paid you a set sum every year for ever. No interaction at all was required for the former and only a couple of hours for the latter. Ordinary people did not have to engage – and so they didn't. That's changed. There is no set sum. There is only a fund filled with mostly shares that is not generally swapped for an annuity and which has to provide an income for ever. That means that we have no choice but to be the protectors of our own investments, both as we save and as we run down our savings. It also means that all age groups are forced to engage and reinvent the social contract with big companies along the way.

These changes might happen quite fast. How? There is a hint of improvement in announcements from BlackRock over the last couple of years. Having long said that giving its clients the right to directly use the votes of the shares held on their behalf was just too difficult and expensive, the firm has now changed its mind. In October 2021, they announced that clients holding some $4.8tn-worth of assets with BlackRock would now get to vote. This doesn't do quite what we want: it only transfers the vote from BlackRock to other asset managers, rather than to the real individual owners of the assets. However, it is useful in that it shows that the technology exists to make passing voting rights down the ownership pyramid both inexpensive and more straightforward than before.

More interesting, however, for the purposes of real shareholder democracy, is that there is a fabulous newish company – one I mentioned in the last chapter – working on getting the vote directly to individuals in exactly the way we want. In 2020, voter choice software firm Tumelo, founded by Georgia Stewart, teamed up with Legal & General Investment Management (LGIM). Using Tumelo's software, the agreement effectively allows 52,000 investors with LGIM to visit the LGIM site, look at a list of all the companies they hold via their funds and also see what shareholder votes are coming up for those companies.

They can see the arguments for both sides and then share how they would use their vote (were it legally theirs). They then get to see how other investors would vote, how LGIM does vote and the final outcome of the vote. The idea, said LGIM at the time, was to "provide members with greater transparency… as well as to increase their engagement on the way their money is managed, through a greater understanding of the sensitive decision-making process of companies in which they own a stake". This is not perfect. It is only advisory, not binding, and has "no direct impact on the vote indications set by LGIM's stewardship team" (although LGIM does commit to explain why, if it has voted against the majority opinion). LGIM also isn't thinking of splitting its votes to reflect investor opinion – its entire stake is voted one way and one way only. But that aside, it seems promising. LGIM noted in March 2021 that some 6,000 people have voted once and that a good 50% had returned to vote again. And the most interested group? Those aged between 25 and 35.

This is great news for LGIM – its clients are already suggesting that they are more likely to top up their pension if they know what is in it and see it as actual companies they recognise rather than just a pile of incomprehensible acronyms. In a world where we need people to save, says LGIM, this is a "hidden superpower in the market". It's also great for the end investors. You might think all this clicking and voting is pandering to the gamification of the stock market for the young, but if it gives people the voice they should have, how could that be a bad thing? Remember the story of McDonald's and its study into antibiotic use I told in Chapter 6? If you'd been with a fund manager that worked with Tumelo you could have had your say on what happened next. At LGIM, 52,000 people had the opportunity to have their say. Not all used it, of course – but they could have. LGIM is the trailblazer here but other organisations are getting the idea. UK pensions start-up Penfold is also working with Tumelo on a "Have Your Say Dashboard" which works in much the same way – allowing investors a say on everything from the antibiotics issue to whether Amazon should be asked by its shareholders to report on its use of plastics. This is a large part of the solution to the asset manager capitalism problem. Sure, you could just write to your fund manager every week or so and tell them how you feel about any issues. But we all know you probably won't. Instead, why not write just one letter to your fund manager and ask them to talk to Tumelo. Then once they are all set up, ask them when your suggestion as to how they should vote is going to be more binding than advisory. This initiative is key. It shows that the technology is easily available for us to be allowed to use the votes (even the fractions of votes) attached to our shares held in their funds. One to push for.

Finally, we might ask those who say we won't use our votes to look again at the whole Robinhood and GameStop saga. Whatever your views on it, it proved one thing to the corporate world: if retail investors club together they have astonishing power over the financial world. Perhaps the thing that many will remember from 2020 and 2021 is not the frenzy of fractional share trading and mobile apps but the revelation that ordinary people can control real stakes in real companies. Companies and journalists might be overestimating the importance of the rise of the retail investor in the very short term, but I bet most are underestimating it in the long term. GameStop could, as Robin Wrigglesworth, commented in the *Financial Times*, be "emblematic of an inflection point for financial markets – where the whims of retail investors might start to matter a little more".[131] I hope so.

Imagine, I said in one of my *Financial Times* columns in early 2021, that instead of just amusing themselves pissing off hedge funds by playing with the GameStop share price, a group called r/shareholderdemocracyaction on Reddit had noticed that General Electric chief executive Larry Culp (who we met in Chapter 6), was in line for an outrageous $47m bonus if the company's share price hit $10 – and urged "swarms" of small investors to prevent it doing so. That would send a genuine message about social justice expectations to grotesquely overpaid CEOs everywhere. Or imagine if 4.8 million investors turned up at GE's next virtual AGM to use their votes – and to complain about the $230m Mr Culp would have got if the price went to

$16.68. Now that would make a difference. Then there is Extinction Rebellion. Imagine if, instead of wasting the world's resources by smashing windows in the City that then have to be replaced, they bought a share each (I don't think a share often costs more than a hammer of glass-breaking quality) and submitted a few useful resolutions. Less fun. Also more effective.

There are precedents for buying a few shares and turning up to make a fuss at company meetings. In the US, there is a long history of orders of nuns teaming up to submit resolutions at company meetings (in the US you need to have held $2,000 worth of shares for a year to be able to do so at the moment).[132] This, says Sister Sandra Sherman, president of the Ursuline Convent of the Sacred Heart in Toledo, has long allowed her and her community to "engage with companies on critical issues". This lot, notes the *New York Times*, were totally on top of shareholder activism long before Occupy Wall Street even existed.[133] Even more famous than the nuns, however, are the Gilbert brothers, the original champions of what they called corporate democracy. Their family fortune was made in the California Gold Rush (their great-grandparents sold the pickaxes, pots and pans the miners needed). That fortune was shifted into stock markets, and in the 1930s brothers Lewis and John started to attend shareholder meetings. And complain. A lot. Furious at the lack of attention paid to individual shareholders, they soon upped the ante – attending 150 meetings a year and asking all the questions CEOs didn't want to answer. They even founded their own non-profit organisation (Corporate Democracy, Inc) and published (until 1979) an annual report that covered the matters they raised at all these meetings. When thwarted, Lewis was keen to point out to chairmen: "YOU WORK FOR ME." The world needs more Gilberts.

In the UK, there is ShareAction, which holds shares in some of the world's biggest companies across the UK and Europe – and uses those shares to go to AGMs and ask questions to challenge management on "the issues that matter". These companies rely on our savings being invested in them to function, says ShareAction, "so we should have a voice". In the UK, a group of just 100 share-holders (who only need hold one share each) is enough to force a company to put a resolution to all shareholders. So in March 2021, ShareAction orchestrated 100 people to use their shares to force Tesco to put a resolution to share-holders at its next AGM that would – if passed – require it to disclose targets and progress around encouraging shop-pers to opt for fewer fatty salty and sugary foods. You may or may not approve of this. There are, after all, upsides (less obesity perhaps) and downsides (the more processed the food, the higher the margins for the supermarkets – less of it means less profit). But that's not the point. The point is that shareholders have the ability to make a difference on this kind of issue. And not only at the AGM. After the forcing of the resolution, Tesco pledged to aim to lift the proportion of "healthy products" it sells from 58% of total sales to 65% and to quadruple sales of plant-based alternatives to meat by 2025. Tesco said it had been moving in this direction anyway. ShareAction said it was "crystal clear" the move had been taken because of the resolution. The more companies think votes will be used, the more they will react to them. Engagement, says ShareAction's CEO Catherine Howarth, should not be an "elite sport". Quite right. We shouldn't be completely comfortable with the likes of ShareAction. They don't necessarily have a significant stake in the financial futures of the companies they target – and their interest is more activism than shareholder value (although they would say the two are one). But they do demonstrate just how effective smaller shareholders can be if they want to make a noise.

The other good news, as discussed in Chapter 4, is that there has been progress in bringing new firms to market. In the US, the list of those companies that came to market in 2020 was pretty thrilling. Think Airbnb, Lyft, Doordash, Uber, Snowflake. In all, $149bn was raised by companies listing their shares in the US.[134] That's the most since 2014 – despite the world basically stopping in 2020. The UK also saw a spate of great listings – real fast-growing companies in important sectors rather than, as was the case in the last IPO (initial public offering) boom time of 1999, silly word combos with dotcom at the end. This is vital. Everyone should get a chance to invest in newish and growing companies. It helps with engagement if exciting companies are coming to market. It's easier to get people to feel interested in renewables, life sciences and technology than in, say, brick making. But new listings are also a crucial part of shareholder democracy: who cares about voting if there are no companies offering issues to vote on? There's also much discussion globally about making listing easier for founders. In the UK, for example, there is a move afoot to allow companies with dual shareholding structures – in which founders get to hang on to special shares with extra voting powers – into the main index (something other countries already allow). Not everyone likes the idea of this – after all, one of the points of shareholder democracy is one share, one vote. But there are also good arguments for it. If there are a lot of high-growth companies looking for somewhere to list but led by founders who are nervous of ceding full control of their babies on going public – partly on the basis that they know their companies best – why should they not be accommodated? That's particularly the case if we time-limit the extra rights on the special shares – perhaps they can expire after five years.

This is not just about the number of new shares being listed, though. It is about access to those listings. In 2020, the vast majority of companies that came to the market to sell shares to either raise extra money (when they were already listed) or to list for the first time, bypassed individual investors in favour of institutions. Why? Getting to the thousands of ordinary individuals out there was too hard, they said. In the unprecedented circumstances of Covid, said companies, the complicated admin would have slowed things down, and that just wouldn't do. This was nonsense, of course. Time wasn't that critical, and companies had been ignoring small investors for many years before Covid. In the three years prior to March 2021, there was no allocation of shares to retail investors in 93% of the major IPOs in the UK. There was none in Dr Martens and none in Moonpig (both of which listed in the UK in 2021). This isn't allowed everywhere – in Hong Kong and Australia, for example, there has to be an offering to retail. And it is now beginning to shift in the UK too. Not only have the platforms been fairly vocal on the matter (IPOs provide great marketing opportunities for them) but the technology exists to allow companies to sell direct to individual investors anyway. Enter Primary Bid, a newish company that can take away most of the complications. As a retail investor, you can download their app and, thanks to their deal with the London Stock Exchange, you should be on the list to get an immediate push notification when an offering is under way. You can then see all the same documentation as institutional investors, use your debit card to apply for shares and have them settled to whichever investment platform you use. Not slow, not complicated.

All this is very positive. The retail investor has been ignored for years – which is wrong. After all, we are the end owners of the majority of shares. But times have changed. The technology now exists for us to have low-cost, fully transparent access to our own voting rights. The industry and regulators are beginning to recognise this, but there is still a very long way to go.

8

THE WAY FORWARD

The key point I have been trying to make for the last seven chapters is this: if we are to have our say over the future of our economy, we need to do more to reunite owners of equities with the rights of ownership of equities. This process is beginning. We have new investors, ones who may well stick the course. When individual investors last went mad for the market, it was during the dotcom boom. Then, their average age was around 50, they had tens of thousands of dollars to play with – and when they lost it, they left the market to try and rebuild their retirement funds elsewhere. The new entrants this time round are more likely to stay in. Those who are in because they have been auto-enrolled into pension funds haven't really got a choice. And the newcomers who started trading for fun during the pandemic might have more longevity than you think. They are young. They seem unfazed by losses, have more time and, you know, YOLO.[135] If trading is slick, easy and comes with no commission, if you can do it on the bus or in a café at lunch, if you can get all the information you think you need from social media, and if you have a long-term bias, why stop? The new investors might not be as active as they were in the otherwise dull months of lockdown, but they nonetheless represent a generation that has come to investing early – and are enthusiastic. In a poll from Barclays in July 2021, well over three quarters of UK investors said they intended to continue their lockdown investing habits. Trading and investing have been democratised and gamified, to the extent that anyone can do it. And that should be seen as a good thing. After all, there is power in the numbers of new investors and if they can find a route to use their collective might, there are world-changing times ahead. In a large number of smaller companies in particular, votes over only 5% or so of a company are enough to give shareholders the power to demand change.

This is no longer a question of technology; it is simply a matter of institutional and regulatory will. Institutional support is definitely on the up. One nice example: in February 2021, the UK trade body, the association of investment companies (AIC), launched a Shareholder Engagement Award, the idea being to encourage investment platforms (which collectively in the UK represent around £210bn of shareholder assets – according to

Platforum) to help the shareholders using them to exercise their rights,[136] in particular their rights to vote to attend AGMs and to participate in corporate actions. The easier investment companies make it – and the better the access they provide to data such as annual reports and so on – the more likely they are to win. The AIC has a particular type of company in mind (the listed investment companies they represent) but this is the kind of initiative that will make the difference across the board. We also saw in the last chapter how the regulators are gradually coming round to the idea that what actual owners – or end beneficiaries – want does matter.

What, then, should we be asking of the regulators, of our listed companies and of our fund managers? Here are six ideas.

1. Let us use our votes! The first thing is to persevere with making it easy for individual investors to get and use their vote and to be in direct contact with the companies in which they hold those shares. One share, one easily accessible vote. The second is to push on with transferring some of the rights of ownership to those who own their shares via funds of some sort or another. The Tumelo initiative is exactly the kind of thing I have in mind here.

2. More information. Every fund manager should be

sending their clients transparent information on their holdings as well as on how they have voted on all the resolutions open to them on a regular basis. You can usually find stewardship and voting records on fund manager websites. But why should you have to look? They should also be telling every end client exactly what they have in their portfolios (however many hundreds of companies that involves), what those companies do and what votes are coming up that might affect how they do it. They should then be asking them how they would vote and taking that properly into account – and explaining why they vote differently if they do. Agree or explain. In an ideal world, end owner votes would become binding. Fund managers would have to act on them.

3. Physical AGMs and shareholder perks. It might also be a fun time to bring back shareholder perks – at least for those who vote. In the old days, shareholders would head off to AGMs for a free pen and biscuit, and shareholders in some companies were also entitled to discounts on products made by or provided by the firms in which they held shares.[137] A little incentive never goes amiss. AGMs are another obvious place to start. In 2020, almost all AGMs were closed to physical investors (fine under the circumstances). But in the UK, some 30 companies also offered no way at

all for retail investors to participate (not fine). Since then, as discussed in the last chapter, companies have started to realise that the online infrastructure actually allows them to have very inclusive AGMs (communicate them correctly and suddenly you've got thousands and thousands of attendees) and also provides a great way to offer everyone company updates and Q&As with managers. All good. Going forward, it should be mandatory for all companies to have very well-advertised physical AGMs. Some people like to attend in person – and virtual ones will never work for shareholders such as the Sisters of St Francis of Philadelphia who say they "want to look people in the eye when we ask our question and we want to see that person when they answer". Fair enough – and a biscuit is always nice too. However, it should also be mandatory to livestream them and to allow all online participants the right to fully participate (including those who hold their shares inside a fund).

4. Make listing easier. This could all be a bit tiring for companies – and the last thing we want is to put them off listing, just when, as discussed in Chapter 7, they are beginning to want to come back to the market. So alongside measures letting the world's listed companies know they have to listen to owners, we need to make it worth their while to bother listing

in the first place.[138] How? We could start with an overhaul of the relentless regulation and cost that put them off – particularly for smaller companies. No annual report needs 50,000 words. My *MoneyWeek* colleague Matthew Lynn puts this well. Over the last 30 years, he says, "we have introduced a new code for quoted companies to follow on average every two years. There are guidelines on when financial statements need to be published, and in what form, and when and how you can release them to the public. There are rules on who sits on the board, and how much they can be paid, and now there has to be the right number of women as well. Pay scales have to be monitored, and length of service. There is almost no decision a quoted company can make without having to check it complies with one of the codes." That makes being listed very hard indeed. We can make it a little easier. That might also involve pushing ahead with some of the easing of listing rules discussed in the last chapter – allowing founders bringing their companies to market to hold extra voting shares for the first three years, for example.[139] If they can't quite bring themselves to hand something they have created from scratch straight over to the vagaries of the stock market all in one go, why should we not humour them, particularly if it means we get access to a sliver of the growth they are creating along the way? We might also look at the interaction between companies and investors when they do list. In a normal listing (or what is normal at the moment), the investment banks manage things, charging a fortune for figuring out and underwriting what they believe to be the correct price for the shares and then placing them directly with the institutions. Individual investors rarely get a look in – they can buy after the shares hit the market, but they effectively come to the market already owned by the big asset managers. One way to change this is by offering direct allocations to private investors – as was commonplace even 30 years ago. Ocado offered shares to customers when it listed in 2010. The maximum you could buy was £12,000. By January 2021, after a year of everyone wanting home delivery, you would have made 10 times that – and, I suspect, developed a nice sense of long-term loyalty to the firm! There is also the possibility of offering all the shares you are listing to everyone (bypassing the investment banks). In 2018, Spotify went public in New York and did just so by placing a large number of shares on the market and waiting for people to buy them. No hoopla required. The shares found their own level (without expensive investment banker input) and that was that. This is called a direct listing – there should be more of them.

5. Change the tax system. There is also an excellent case to be made for making some dramatic changes to the tax system. Taking out debt is currently treated much more favourably by the system than selling new shares to raise money. This kind of tax favouritism incentivises the former over the latter. It has also been a huge force behind the private equity boom – which is mainly driven by cheap debt. The system can be changed (by any government willing to stand up to the many lobbyists who don't want it changed). However, given the huge long-term social and economic value of companies being listed (and us knowing they are listed and effectively community owned) rather than private, we should also be talking about offering listed companies tax breaks to get them to market. Perhaps a lower corporation tax rate for the first three years of being listed? Or a lower rate charged to all smaller companies listing? Again, this isn't hard – and could be completely transformative. The same goes for tax breaks on capital gains for founders who list. In some countries, you do get some kind of tax break on selling companies – as a reward for entrepreneurship – but you get it regardless of who you sell to. How about shifting that so it only counts if your gains come from listing?[140]

6. Make a director care. One thing we could easily

regulate for – with no obvious downside – is for all companies to have one non-executive director who is responsible for engagement with end beneficiaries – us – not with the big fund managers (there's plenty of this already).

None of these things are going to happen overnight – there's a lot of work to be done on the plumbing of the system, if nothing else. But the last year has shown that shareholder democracy is very far from dead. We've seen a wave of both new listings and new investors. The equity markets are back on form, bringing together those who are building or running businesses and need capital and those who have it to offer. The vast majority of people living in developed countries are in one way or another owners of capital and hence of companies – be it via a fractional stock held in Robinhood or a long-term holding in a pension they don't yet quite understand they have. That makes now the perfect time to work on making things better. It's also a perfect time to start providing a little education on these vitally important matters in schools. There is much momentum behind the idea that personal finance should be taught as part of the curriculum, but none of the material I have seen surrounding this discusses the subject of this book. It should. Young people are the ones with the energy to demand change – we should give them the tools.

So what can you do while you wait? Write to your

platform asking them to make it easier for you to vote. Write to the politician who represents you asking them to take some action. Write to the managers of all the funds where you have units, asking them to set up some Tumelo-style software so you can get going on engaging. Let them know what you think – firmly is fine. Good managers will eventually grasp that this is one of the greatest marketing opportunities ever ("we give our clients a voice") and move fast. There'll be a fabulous first-mover advantage here. And if you have individual shares you can vote, use them (even if you have to do a little admin first). Use the rights you have already, and demand the ones you should have – then use them too. You could also work on your employer. It is your employer who chooses where to auto-enrol your pension contributions and the default fund they end up in. That gives them huge power. This power is starting to be used a little around the world (in France, an employer with more than 50 employees has to offer "solidarity funds" which allocate 10% of the money in them to investments that come with some kind of social or environmental purpose). But it should be used more: how brilliant would it be if, rather than just going through the motions of choosing something that sounds good for us, they selected an institution or fund that might also give us our voices back? The CEOs of BlackRock, State Street and Vanguard are not actually kings of the world. It is up us to remind them of this.

If we can do all this and in doing it make sure everyone knows they have a stake in the system and some influence over it, the future will contain not just the kind of prosperity that free market capitalism always brings, but the kind of inclusive capitalism we can all get behind. Capitalism is good. Shareholder capitalism is better.

Glossary

Active investing: creating a flexible portfolio by carefully selecting individual stocks, regardless of how they are represented in an index, with the clear aim of beating the average returns of the market.

Annual General Meeting (AGM): all companies have a meeting every year at which the shareholders and directors meet. Shareholders get the opportunity to ask questions and to vote on key issues such as the election of directors and auditors.

Annual report: every year companies produce and make available to their shareholders a report that runs through their performance over the previous year, the general condition of their business and their expectations for the future. The report is audited by the firm's accountants. These reports are generally very long, jammed with information included for regulatory purposes and quite boring. However, if you want to understand the detail of a business, the annual report is a very good place to start.

Asset allocation: the process of deciding how to divide

your investments up between the different asset groups — usually equities, bonds, property, commodities and cash.

Bear market: one in which share prices fall by 20% or more. Opposite of a bull market!

Blue chip: a big, well-established and well-known company considered to be high quality — and hence reasonably low risk for investors.

Bond: an IOU issued by a company or a government. You buy the bond and the company or state promises to pay you an annual rate of interest for a certain number of years and then to return your capital to you at the end of the arranged term. You can sell the bond on the open market before it is redeemed. If interest rates fall, it will be worth more (your rate of interest is higher than that being offered by the market) and, if they rise, it will be worth less (your rate is lower than that offered by the market).

Bull market: one in which prices are rising — and have been for some time. A bull market doesn't come with the same precise definition as a bear market (prices down 20%).

Company: complicated — see Chapter 1.

Dividend: the share of a company's profits paid out to shareholders. These can be expressed as absolute amounts or as a percentage of the share price (the percentage is known as the dividend yield). Dividends are what make it worth holding shares in companies even if they aren't growing very fast. Cash is always nice to have.

Extraordinary General Meeting (EGM): a meeting between the shareholders and directors of a company other than the scheduled AGM.

Equity: the same as a share (see page 149). A security that represents ownership of a fraction of a company.

Exchange Traded Fund (ETF): a bundled basket of shares or other securities traded on a stock exchange. These are a bit like a fund but can be traded all day as if they were a share. Mostly used by passive investors.

Expense ratio: the cost of holding an investment fund expressed as a percentage of the total value of the assets held by the fund.

FTSE 100: an index tracking the performance of the biggest 100 listed companies in the UK.

Growth investing: an investment strategy that focuses on buying only fast-growing companies (often at what look like high prices).

Impact investing: a style of investing that aims to create some kind of real positive impact (usually social or environmental) as well as a financial return.

Index: an index tracks the performance of a basket of securities (of any kind) with a view to measuring its overall performance. There are thousands of indices in use in the investing world, but most often you will hear of indices such as the FTSE 100, which tracks the performance of the UK's largest listed companies or the S&P 500, which tracks the largest 500 listed companies in the US.

Initial Public Offering (IPO): the act of raising money by listing and selling shares in a company via a public stock exchange for the first time.

Investment fund: a collective vehicle for investing. Everyone hands their money over in exchange for units in the fund and the whole lot is run by a fund manager. Sometimes well. Sometimes badly.

Individual Savings Account (ISA): a tax-efficient savings wrapper available to UK residents (you can save both cash and shares into these).

JISA: junior version of the above – available up to the age of 18.

Large cap: short hand for a very big company (with a high market value or "capitalisation"). You will also hear talk of mid caps and small caps.

Management fee: the fee an investment manager takes from an investment fund every year.

Passive investing: buying a group of shares or an investment with a view to merely replicating the average performance of an index. This takes little skill, does not require an active portfolio manager and can therefore be very cost effective.

Pension wrapper: a pension is not a thing in itself – it is just a collection of investments. When we refer to a pension, we are normally referring to the tax-protective wrapper these investments are in. Think of the wrapper like a box in which you store the actual investments – as long as they stay in there, you pay no tax on the capital gains or dividends they produce. We also talk about ISA wrappers.

Platform: an online service that allows you to buy sell and hold shares bonds and funds in a personal account.

Portfolio: the collection of investments owned by an individual or a fund.

Proxy vote: a vote cast by someone else on your behalf.

Resolution: a resolution is a proposal submitted by the board or shareholders to be voted on at an AGM. The board tends to produce most of these but shareholders are also able to file resolutions and force a vote on them.

Retail investor: individual investor.

S&P 500: an index tracking the performance of the biggest 500 companies in the US.

Secondary listing: the act of raising money via the

issuing of new shares when a company's shares are already listed.

Shares: a share is a unit of ownership in a company. Owning a share means that you have voting rights (one share, one vote) over issues raised at company annual general meetings (AGMs). You also have the right to share in any profits distributed by the company

Shareholder: the owner of a share.

Stock market: a platform on which shares are issued and then bought and sold. Also referred to as a stock exchange.

The agency problem: a conflict of interest that happens when one person is acting as an agent for others (the owners or principals) but has a differing set of incentives to them. Shareholders (principals) hire managers (agents) to run businesses for them.

Value investing: the strategy of buying cheap-looking equities at below what the investor believes to be their true market value.

Votes: most ordinary shares in most companies come with a vote, which the shareholder can use to vote on resolutions at AGMs and EGMs.

401(k) plan: a workplace-provided, tax-efficient pension wrapper available in the US.

Acknowledgements

I had been thinking about the ideas in this book for a few years. Nothing quite happened for the simple reason that I did not want to write a long book. There are too many long books around – and I suspect very few are read cover to cover. Why waste paper? My first thanks must therefore go to Rebecca Nicolson and to Short Books – for existing and for allowing me to write a short book quite fast. Of course, I couldn't have managed even that many without the wonderful editors who made the draft into a book, Helena Sutcliffe and Kate Hubbard.

I'm also hugely grateful to the many people I have discussed this with over the years – Gillian Tett, Claer Barrett, Richard Wilson, Francesca Fairbairn, Anna Macdonald, John Stepek, Heather McGregor, Simon Boote, Russell Napier and many others (I've been talking about it for a while...).

A special thanks also goes to my old friends James Lewisohn and Nick Reid, both for always being there to explain exactly why I am wrong about almost everything and for their forensic proofreading (although any remaining mistakes are mine, as they will no doubt point out when they are found). For introducing me to Rebecca – there was never going to be a long book – John Micklethwait. For making sure everyone can understand the stuff I write, my family and Julie Slack in particular (I think she actually read it).

And finally, of course, for his endless patience with me and for the open access to all the ideas in his head, Sandy.

References

1   https://www.companybug.com/
     how-many-limited-companies-are-there-in-the-uk/
2   www.census.gov
3   John Micklethwait & Adrian Wooldridge, *The Company*,
     Weidenfeld & Nicolson, 2003, p.13
4   Note that shares are still often referred to as stocks.
5   https://en.wikipedia.org/wiki/Bazacle_Milling_Company
6   More detail: http://blog.yalebooks.com/2015/08/11/the-
     worlds-first-corporations-mills-in-fourteenth-century-toulouse/,
     and a whole book: https://yalebooks.yale.edu/search?field_
     book_disciplines=All&field_book_subdisciplines=All&search_
     api_views_fulltext=origins+of+corporations&sort=se
     arch_api_relevance+DESC&sort=search_api_relevance+DESC
7   https://som.yale.edu/news/2014/08/the-fascinating-600-year-
     history-of-french-mill-the-world-s-oldest-shareholding-company
8   https://www.ofgem.gov.uk/data-portal/
     electricity-supply-market-shares-company-domestic-gb
9   Adam Smith, *Wealth of Nations*, W. Strahan and T. Cadell, 1776
10   The South Sea Company was a state-backed trading company.
11   Micklethwait & Wooldridge, op. cit., p.66
12   https://www.carnegie.org/interactives/foundersstory/#!/
13   https://en.wikipedia.org/wiki/U.S._Steel#History
14   https://www.johnkay.com/2018/05/03/theories-of-the-firm/
15   https://www.oecd.org/corporate/who-are-the-owners-of-the-
     worlds-listed-companies-and-why-should-we-care.htm
16   https://www.johnkay.com/2018/05/03/theories-of-the-firm/
17   Yes, the same question is raised in the thought experiment of the
     ship of Theseus. See also Trigger's broom in *Only Fools and Horses*.
18   Jonathan Tepper with Denise Hearn, *The Myth of Capitalism:
     Monopolies and the Death of Competition*, Wiley, 2018
19   https://www.investopedia.com/news/apple-now-bigger-these-5-things

20   https://www.nysscpa.org/news/publications/the-trusted-professional/article/more-americans-work-at-big-firms-than-small-ones-040717

21   https://www.mckinsey.com/featured-insights/innovation-and-growth/what-every-ceo-needs-to-know-about-superstar-companies?cid=other-soc-twi-mip-mck-oth-1904&kui=ucl8P4Qn8qq4dtBYYumDng

22   https://www.oxera.com/wp-content/uploads/2018/03/The-Thatcher-privatisation-legacy_1.pdf

23   John Littlewood, *The Stock Market*, Financial Times Management, 1998, p. 228

24   https://www.schroders.com/en/insights/economics/global-britain-should-the-dramatic-shift-in-ownership-of-the-uk-stock-market-be-feared-or-cheered/

25   Littlewood, op. cit., p. 427

26   Littlewood, ibid., p. 426

27   Rana Foroohar, *Financial Times*, 8/2/21, https://www.pewresearch.org/fact-tank/2020/03/25/more-than-half-of-u-s-households-have-some-investment-in-the-stock-market/

28   https://www.gov.uk/government/statistics/workplace-pension-participation-and-savings-trends-2009-to-2020/workplace-pension-participation-and-savings-trends-of-eligible-employees-2009-to-2020

29   https://assets.publishing.service.gov.uk/government/uploads/system/uploads/attachment_data/file/894771/ISA_Statistics_Release_June_2020.pdf

30   https://www.financemagnates.com/forex/brokers/exclusive-etoro-ended-2020-with-600-million-in-revenue/

31   https://www.nytimes.com/2020/07/08/technology/robinhood-risky-trading.html

32   https://www.wsj.com/articles/companies-zoom-in-on-small-shareholders-amid-retail-trading-frenzy-11614607215

33   https://www.nikkoam.com.hk/articles/2021/japan-equity-monthly-february-2021

34   *Financial Times*, 29/4/21, p. 11

35   https://assets.publishing.service.gov.uk/government/uploads/system/uploads/attachment_data/file/966133/UK_Listing_Review_3_March.pdf

36   New investors in 2020 were far more likely to get their investing ideas from social media than older investors: https://www.cnbc.com/2021/08/23/

invest-in-you-next-gen-survey-finds-behaviors-of-new-investors-are-vastly-different-from-experienced-investors.html

37 https://www.tiktok.com/@pricelesstay?lang=en&is_copy_url=1&is_from_webapp=v1

38 https://moneyweek.com/investments/investment-strategy/602171/cash-rich-and-bored-be-careful-what-you-do-with-your-money

39 https://www.bnymellonwealth.com/insights/the-rise-of-retail-traders.html

40 At some point in 2020, Credit Suisse estimated that one third of trading in the US was by ordinary investors rather than by institutions: https://www.ft.com/content/7a91e3ea-b9ec-4611-9a03-a8dd3b8bddb5

41 https://papers.ssrn.com/sol3/papers.cfm?abstract_id=3776874

42 According to a Deutsche Bank survey quoted in the *Financial Times*, 10/3/21

43 In 2020, 10% of established investors in the UK were furloughed, almost 20% of new investors were: https://audience.findoutnow.co.uk/files/Retail%20Investment%20Boom%20-%20Boscobel%20Partners.pdf

44 https://www.visualcapitalist.com/one-year-in-did-people-save-more-or-less-during-the-pandemic/

45 This process has now begun: https://www.reuters.com/markets/wealth/retail-inflows-nearly-all-time-high-despite-market-turbulence-2022-05-25/

46 *The Times*, 14/5/21

47 Quoted in *The Sunday Times*, 31/1/21: https://www.thetimes.co.uk/article/meet-the-amateur-stock-jocks-flooding-the-market-in-lockdown-3fhfkl585

48 https://news.gallup.com/poll/268295/support-government-inches-not-socialism.aspx

49 https://www.pewresearch.org/fact-tank/2019/07/30/two-thirds-of-americans-favor-raising-federal-minimum-wage-to-15-an-hour/

50 https://www.surveymonkey.com/curiosity/axios-capitalism-update/; https://news.gallup.com/poll/268766/socialism-popular-capitalism-among-young-adults.aspx

51 http://fs2.american.edu/dfagel/www/OwnershipSmaller.pdf

52 https://www.johnkay.com/2015/11/11/is-it-meaningful-to-talk-about-the-ownership-of-companies/

53 https://www.jstor.org/stable/3114162?seq=1

54 Janette Rutterford and Dimitris P. Sotiropoulos, The Rise of the

Small Investor in the US and the UK, 1895 to 1970, *Enterprise & Society*, 2017, 18(3), pp. 485–535.

55 Littlewood, op. cit., p. 442

56 https://www.schroders.com/en/sysglobalassets/digital/insights/2020/november/global-britain/2020-november-stock-market-ownership.pdf

57 http://www.law.harvard.edu/programs/olin_center/papers/pdf/Bebchuk_1004.pdf

58 Littlewood, op. cit.

59 https://www.oecd.org/finance/Financial-markets-insurance-pensions-inclusiveness-and-finance.pdf

60 https://www.oecd.org/corporate/Owners-of-the-Worlds-Listed-Companies.pdf

61 J. Fichtner, E. Heemskerk, and J. Garcia-Bernardo, Hidden power of the Big Three? Passive index funds, re-concentration of corporate ownership, and new financial risk. *Business and Politics*, 2017, 19(2), 298-326. doi:10.1017/bap.2017.6

62 https://uploads-ssl.webflow.com/5e2191f00f868d778b89ff85/6064442e5d2ea3622ef1cc4c_CW_AM_Launch%20Essay.pdf

63 From analysis done by Common Wealth, in a great little report, 'Goliath and Goliath': https://uploads-ssl.webflow.com/5e2191f00f868d778b89ff85/6064442e5d2ea3622ef1cc4c_CW_AM_Launch%20Essay.pdf

64 https://www.gsb.stanford.edu/faculty-research/publications/big-thumb-scale-overview-proxy-advisory-industry

65 https://www.ft.com/content/4e4c119a-8c25-11e8-affd-da9960227309 in 2018

66 https://www.epi.org/publication/ceo-compensation-2018/

67 https://www.gsb.stanford.edu/faculty-research/publications/big-thumb-scale-overview-proxy-advisory-industry

68 https://www.statista.com/statistics/324547/uk-number-of-companies-lse/

69 The Listing Gap, NBER, https://www.nber.org/system/files/working_papers/w21181/w21181.pdf

70 Alexander Ljungqvist & Lars Persson & Joacim Tåg, Private Equity's Unintended Dark Side: On the Economic Consequences of Excessive Delistings, NBER Working Papers 21909, 2016, National Bureau of Economic Research, Inc.

71 *MoneyWeek*, 15/3/19, p. 5

72 Alexander Ljungqvist, Lars Persson and Joacim Tag: https://www.researchgate.net/

73   publication/301231830_The_Incredible_Shrinking_Stock_
Market_On_the_Political_Economy_Consequences_of_
Excessive_Delistings

73   John Kay, *Prospect*, April 2021

74   https://www.nber.org/system/files/working_papers/w21181/
w21181.pdf

75   https://www.morganstanley.com/
im/publication/insights/articles/
articles_publictoprivateequityintheusalongtermlook_us.pdf

76   Gillian Tett, *Financial Times*, 31/5/19

77   Firms that run funds designed to hold and manage private
companies.

78   When interest rates are low in general, governments don't have to
pay much interest to get you to buy their bonds.

79   https://cdn.roxhillmedia.com/production/email/attachment/10
70001_1080000/057f5b1ba5dbcbc8f3763ba4850107facdc57030.
pdf

80   https://www.businessinsider.com/fordlandia-henry-ford-city-
brazil-rainforest-ghost-town-photos-2018-12?r=US&IR=T).

81   Kay, op. cit., April 2021

82   https://www.pwc.com/us/en/services/deals/capital-markets-
watch-quarterly.html

83   SPACs have no underlying business of their own – they are just
raising capital with a view to using it to merge with a private
company – the idea being to end up with that private company
being listed faster than would have been possible otherwise.

84   https://www.nytimes.com/1970/09/13/archives/a-friedman-
doctrine-the-social-responsibility-of-business-is-to.html

85   https://www.coalitionforinclusivecapitalism.com/epic/

86   https://www.businessroundtable.org

87   https://www.thebritishacademy.ac.uk/publications/
reforming-business-21st-century-framework-future-corporation/

88   https://www.unpri.org/pri/
what-are-the-principles-for-responsible-investment

89   *MoneyWeek* podcast, 23/4/21

90   https://www.im.natixis.com/us/resources/2021-esg-investor-
insights-report-executive-overview https://www.im.natixis.com/
intl/research/esg-investing-survey-insights-report

91   *Financial Times*, 25/2/19, p. 9

92   https://www.cnbc.com/2018/01/16/sam-zell-BlackRock-ceo-
fink-is-hypocritical-to-push-social-responsibility.html

93   *Financial Times*, 30/01/21, Life & Arts
94   Rebecca Henderson, *Reimaginging Capitalism*, Penguin Books, 2020
95   https://www.morningstar.co.uk/uk/news/201590/surge-in-funds-rebranding-as-sustainable.aspx
96   https://eu.usatoday.com/story/opinion/2021/03/16/wall-street-esg-sustainable-investing-greenwashing-column/6948923002/
97   https://www.jpmorganchase.com/content/dam/jpmc/jpmorgan-chase-and-co/investor-relations/documents/ceo-letter-to-share-holders-2020.pdf
98   https://www.standard.co.uk/news/uk/body-shop-jk-rowling-transgender-row-twitter-a4465596.html
99   https://nirmalyakumar.com/2018/09/10/yes-nike-great-brands-are-polarizing/
100 Jesse Fried, *Financial Times*, 7/10/19
101 https://www.im.natixis.com/us/resources/2021-esg-investor-insights-report-executive-overview p9
102 https://www.aegon.co.uk/content/ukpaw/news/climate_risk_is_keyconcernforsaversbut.html
103 https://www.im.natixis.com/us/resources/2021-esg-investor-insights-report-executive-overview
104 https://www.telegraph.co.uk/news/2021/07/04/drop-woke-posing-stick-day-job-companies-told/
105 https://www.issgovernance.com/file/publications/iss-sg-themes-trends-2021-global.pdf
106 https://www.ft.com/content/0676c6f6-1ad2-490d-b8cf-d3bccdb76182
107 https://shareaction.org/research-resources/voting-matters-2020/
108 https://www.asiatimesfinancial.com/; https://www.ft.com/content/479b9dd2-c738-4310-8b1e-afdfbd3921b0 activists-accuse-BlackRock-of-palm-oil-hypocrisy
109 Yup, it's BlackRock again! The others were Lyxor, Nordea, Credit Suisse and Ninety One. https://shareaction.org/research-resources/voting-matters-2020/
110 https://www.blackrock.com/corporate/literature/publication/blk-annual-stewardship-report-2020.pdf
111 https://www.thetimes.co.uk/article/76m-builder-jeff-fairburn-is-told-to-put-his-house-in-order-f2xrwwb0p
112 *Financial Times*, 25/2/19
113 https://www.sharesoc.org/blog/retail-shareholder-participation-in-voting-us-study/
114 https://www.ft.com/

content/131f52af-53c5-47d8-b915-767df8403bb5
115 https://money.cnn.com/quote/shareholders/shareholders.html?s
ymb=MCD&subView=institutional
116 https://jpm.pm-research.com/content/35/1/82.abstract
117 https://www.institutionalinvestor.com/article/b1rkzgfmhz1wkr/
Is-ESG-Outperformance-Just-an-Illusion
118 https://friendsoftheearth.uk/climate-change/divestment
119 https://www.ft.com/
content/00d493fe-839d-4575-aedc-a6a7c17169e7
120 https://dispatches.business-humanrights.org/human-rights-in-
the-mineral-supply-chains-of-wind-turbines/index.html
121 https://news.gallup.com/poll/5248/big-business.aspx
122 https://news.gallup.com/poll/268766/socialism-popular-
capitalism-among-young-adults.aspx
123 https://fortune.com/2020/11/15/
citizen-capitalism-accountable-bain-capital-book-esg-investing/
124 https://migrationobservatory.ox.ac.uk/resources/briefings/
uk-public-opinion-toward-immigration-overall-attitudes-and-level-
of-concern/
125 https://www.lebow.drexel.edu/sites/default/files/event/
1579898324-brav-cain-zytnicretail-shareholder-participation-
proxy-process-monitoring-engagement-and-voting.pdf
126 https://corpgov.law.harvard.edu/2020/10/21/back-to-the-
future-reclaiming-shareholder-democracy-through-virtual-annual-
meetings/
127 https://corporate.marksandspencer.com/investors/
shareholder-information/shareholder-panel
128 https://www.unpri.org/download?ac=13321
129 https://www.sec.gov/news/speech/lee-every-vote-counts
130 https://scholarship.law.upenn.edu/cgi/viewcontent.cgi?article
=1581&context=jbl
131 https://www.ft.com/content/af74599a-2344-4a51-ac32-
c299930bcdda
132 https://www.ft.com/content/2bae15d2-bcbf-444a-8d31-
c547ba5197f4
133 https://www.nytimes.com/2011/11/13/business/sisters-of-
st-francis-the-quiet-shareholder-activists.html
134 *Financial Times*, 18/12/20
135 You only live once…
136 https://www.theaic.co.uk/shareholder-engagement-award
137 You can still get these – though not all platforms are great

at passing them on. In 2021, you could get 35% off books at Bloomsbury, 20% off instore at Mulberry and 2% off a new house with Persimmon, for example!

138   In 2021, the UK started a review of its listing rules.

139   https://assets.publishing.service.gov.uk/government/uploads/ system/uploads/attachment_data/file/966133/UK_Listing_ Review_3_March.pdf

140   In the UK, Business Asset Disposal relief can cut your capital gains liability to 10%

About the Author

Merryn Somerset Webb is an award-winning financial commentator and Senior Columnist at Bloomberg. She is the former Editor-in-Chief of *MoneyWeek*, the UK's best-selling financial magazine, and was a Contributing Editor and weekly columnist at the *Financial Times*. Somerset Webb is also a non-executive director of several UK listed investment trusts and a regular media commentator and speaker on all things financial. She lives in Edinburgh.